True Stories From World War I

Peter Hepplewhite is an ex-history teacher who is an education officer at Tyne & Wear Archives Service. He co-wrote *Horrible Histories: Awesome Egyptians* with Terry Deary and has written non-fiction titles for Wayland, Hodder and Hamlyn. He wrote two of the books in the series A World in Flames, about World War II, for Macmillan.

Although **David Wyatt** is primarily known for his work on fiction, including novels by Terry Pratchett and Philip Pullman, he has a love of history and enjoys the education he receives when working on factual projects. He lives on Dartmoor, which is stuffed full of history, as well as amazing landscapes to stimulate his overactive imagination.

True Stories

From

World War I

PETER HEPPLEWHITE

ILLUSTRATIONS AND MAPS BY DAVID WYATT

MACMILLAN CHILDREN'S BOOKS

World War I: On Land and *World War I: In the Air*
first published individually 2003 by Macmillan Children's Books

This edition published 2014 by Macmillan Children's Books
a division of Macmillan Publishers Limited
20 New Wharf Road, London N1 9RR
Basingstoke and Oxford
Associated companies throughout the world
www.panmacmillan.com

ISBN 978-1-4472-5629-8

1 3 5 7 9 8 6 4 2

A CIP catalogue record for this book is available from
the British Library.

Typeset by Nigel Hazle
Printed and bound by CPI Group (UK) Ltd, Croydon CR0 4YY

CONTENTS

REMEMBRANCE

Between 2014 and 2018 Britain is commemorating the First World War. For those alive at the time it had another name: The Great War. Tragically, some forty countries across the globe were involved. The main killing grounds were in Europe, but the conflict spilt out into the Middle East, Africa and across the oceans.

Losses were vast. Around 65 million men joined up and almost 10 million died – an average of 6,000 every day for four and half years. Another 21 million were wounded and, though many recovered, others bore physical or mental damage for the rest of their lives. Nearly 7 million civilians died from disease, starvation or were killed in military operations.

Every British family was affected. Children grew up with fathers away and went to schools stripped of male teachers. Women picked up the pieces in industry and agriculture, trying not to worry about husbands, sons, brothers or fathers fighting abroad. Families lived in dread of receiving Army Form B104–82 – the official notice that someone they loved was missing or killed in action.

With peace came time to grieve. No community was too small to have a war memorial, with a long list of the dead carved in stone. No workplace, school or public building went without a Roll of Honour by the door bearing the names of those killed, perhaps in Flanders, on the Somme or in Gallipoli.

Today there are no surviving combatants of the Great War. Harry Patch, the last veteran who served in the trenches, died in 2009, while Claude Choules, the last sailor, died in 2011. Yet their generation lives on in stories told by millions of modern families. Diaries and letters from the front, pay-books and service bibles, faded photographs of smiling soldiers and sets of medals are treasured keepsakes. The Great War is not forgotten.

This book tries in a small way to join the commemorations with twelve cracking tales of bravery and endurance from that remarkable era.

PART I

STORIES FROM THE LAND

To John Bonallie, for many happy years of jokes and anecdotes. And no, John, I'm not paying you for all those 'useful facts'!

INTRODUCTION

'THE GREAT WAR'

In August 1914 the showdown between the great powers of Europe began. The Allies – Britain, France and Russia – lined up against the Central Powers: Germany and Austria-Hungary. By the end of the year Europeans were already calling this 'the Great War'. No one expected the fighting to be so ferocious and no one could find a way to win. New and terrible weapons, especially artillery, machine guns, aeroplanes and barbed wire, brought a bloody stalemate and the deaths of millions. The killing lasted for four long years.

Alliance Trip Wire 1914
In 1914 most countries in Europe were bound together in tight alliances – so when the fighting began everyone piled in, like a deadly playground scrap. The crisis was

1

triggered by the assassination of Archduke Franz Ferdinand in Sarajevo, Serbia, on 28 June.

- **Thwack!** Franz Ferdinand was the heir to the Austro-Hungarian throne. His death led an outraged Austria-Hungary to declare war on Serbia.
- **Thwack!** Russia, the ally of Serbia, began to **mobilize** a vast army on the Austro-Hungarian and German borders.
- **Thwack!** To hit first, Austria-Hungary's ally, Germany, declared war on Russia and Russia's main partner, France.
- **Thwack!** To knock out France, Germany launched the Schlieffen Plan – a huge attack through neutral Belgium.
- **Thwack!** Britain was dragged into the war to protect Belgium. The British Expeditionary Force (BEF) of 100,000 men left for France.

Hopes of a short, sharp fight were soon dashed as the opposing armies dug in on the Western Front – over 400 miles (600 km) of trenches stretching from the Swiss border to the English Channel. Troops from all over the British Empire – India, Canada, New Zealand and Australia – flocked to Britain's aid, while Algerians and Africans fought alongside the French. Turkey joined the Central Powers.

1915

The Germans tried to break through British lines in Belgium and were the first to use poisonous gas. Stalemate on the Western Front led the Allies to attack Turkey at Gallipoli and Mesopotamia (Iraq). The passenger liner *Lusitania* was sunk by a German **U-boat** off the Irish coast, sparking rage in the USA, because many American civilians drowned. The bloodshed was carried across the Alps when Italy joined the Allies. London suffered its first Zeppelin raid, and aircraft on the Western Front were armed with machine guns – the war had spread to the air. Sir Douglas Haig became commander of the BEF.

1916

By January 1916 2.5 million volunteers had joined the British army, but this was not enough. Conscription was introduced. Germany launched a huge attack against the French at Verdun. In the war at sea, the Royal Navy faced its sternest test since Trafalgar, over a century before: the Battle of Jutland. The result was a draw, but the German High Seas fleet feared another showdown and stayed in port after this. On 1 July 20,000 British soldiers were killed on the first day of the Battle of the Somme, and the fighting there went on until November. Lloyd George took over from Herbert Asquith as British Prime Minister. Hindenburg became the German Chief of Staff.

1917

German U-boats almost cut off British food supplies from North America. The USA entered the war in April, and in November the communists seized power in Russia and sought peace terms from Germany. The British tried to break through enemy lines at Passchendaele with a huge loss of life.

1918

In March Germany launched a massive spring offensive and drove a wedge between the British and French armies. Haig issued his famous 'backs to the wall' order: 'Every position must be held to the last man.' By the end of April this attack was exhausted and the tide slowly turned in favour of the Allies. The last 100 days of the war began on 8 August with a great Allied victory at the Battle of Amiens. The Germans called this 'the Black Day' because they lost 27,000 men in casualties and prisoners. In the weeks that followed British and Empire troops drove the enemy relentlessly back. On 9 November **Kaiser** Wilhelm abdicated. At 11:00 on 11 November the war ended. Cheering crowds danced in the streets of London and Paris.

1919

The Paris Peace Conference led to the Treaty of Versailles. In it, Germany was blamed for the war, lost territory and paid huge compensation to the Allies.

Britain survived but at a heavy cost: 700,000 dead and debts of £1,000 million to the USA (about £1,250 billion today). Paying the interest on this debt took half the nation's taxes during the 1920s and 1930s.

War Stories
This book highlights six stunning stories from this gruelling war and gives you the fighting facts behind them.

- **The Christmas Truce**
  Christmas 1914. Life in the trenches is miserable – cold, wet and extremely dangerous. But then there is hope, in the form of an unofficial ceasefire. But what will the generals say? Bruce Bairnsfather is in the front line on one of the strangest days of the war.

- **An Underground War**
  Mysterious explosions rock the British line from December 1914 – the Germans are using mines. Something must be done, and quickly, but can the 'clay-kickers' (tunnellers) save the day?

- **Gallipoli – a Side Show**
  With the war dragging on in Europe, the Allies are looking for a quick fix. Will an attack against Turkey solve all their problems?

- **Guests of the Kaiser**

  The Canadian Baron Richardson Racey is captured during a German gas attack. Can he escape the grim camps and reach the safety of neutral Holland?

- **The Prisoners' Martyr – Edith Cavell**

  In 1915 Edith Cavell is running an escape network for Allied prisoners in Belgium. Why is the prim and proper daughter of a Norfolk vicar taking such a risk ... and why does she freely admit her actions to the enemy?

- **Aftermath**

  Who is the Unknown Warrior and why is he so important?

If your reading ends up in no man's land, help is at hand. Words shown in **bold** type are explained in Trench Talk or the Glossary on pages 127–30.

Never Mind

If the sergeant drinks your rum, never mind
And your face may lose its smile, never mind
He's entitled to a tot but not the bleeding lot
If the sergeant drinks your rum, never mind.

When old Jerry shells your trench, never mind
And your face may lose its smile, never mind
Though the sandbags burst and fly, you have
    only once to die,
When old Jerry shells your trench, never mind.

If you get stuck on the wire, never mind
And your face may lose its smile, never mind
Though you're stuck there all the day, they
    count you dead and stop your pay
If you get stuck on the wire, never mind.

Trench song

THE CHRISTMAS TRUCE

BATTLE BRIEFING

The Western Front

When World War I broke out in August 1914 the news was greeted by cheering crowds and yells of 'On to Berlin' or 'On to St Petersburg'. Most people believed there would be a decisive battle like Waterloo, a century before, and the troops would be home by Christmas. It wasn't to be.

German hopes lay in the Schlieffen Plan – a mighty right hook through Belgium to get behind the main French army and take Paris. It almost worked. The BEF and the French Fifth Army were hurled back, until a last desperate stand was made on the River Marne. This in turn forced the Germans to retreat and both sides began the so-called 'race to the sea' – fierce and bloody attempts to **outflank** each other and capture the Channel ports.

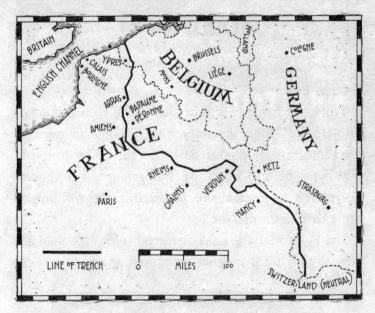

The Western Front, 1914

By November this war of movement was over and opposing trench systems had been dug from the Channel to Switzerland. Early attempts to punch a way through ended in terrible slaughter, as tens of thousands of men fell amid the chatter of machine guns. The pattern of the war was set for the next three and a half years: mud, blood, death and misery.

During the bleak winter of 1914–15 the BEF held the line in Belgium. Among the unlucky soldiers was Bruce Bairnsfather, a machine-gun officer in the Royal Warwickshire Regiment. He had just arrived, fresh and optimistic, from England and was about to get his first taste of trench warfare ... and a very unexpected Christmas.

SILENT NIGHT

Trench Life

Bruce never forgot his first spell in the trenches – few soldiers did. To escape the storm of German guns, his battalion moved up after dusk to a turnip field next to the huge Bois (forest) de Ploegsteert. The British **Tommies** had soon shortened this elegant Belgian name to 'Plugstreet Wood'.

The Plugstreet trenches zigzagged across the field and offered only poor protection against enemy fire. These

Bruce Bairnsfather

A British trench at Messines Ridge, considerably dried and better organized than those experienced by Bruce in 1914

were the 'Mark I trenches', little more than shallow ditches hastily cut into the clay. They had few of the later luxuries of frontline life, such as corrugated-iron sheets for roofing, wooden duckboards to walk on or sandbag supports for the oozing walls. British generals were still sure that they would break through the German lines early in 1915, so what was the point of wasting effort on trenches that would soon be left far behind?

It had been raining dismally for days and the ground was saturated as the Warwickshires sloshed in. Bruce saw to it that his machine guns were set up and gunners settled for the night. This was not easy, since the rain had washed away many of the **dugouts** left by earlier units and they had to be carved out of the slithery mud again. Now it was time for him to try to snatch a damp sleep, but where? Together with his sergeant, Bruce made two shallow caves from the soaking clay, one behind the other, and crawled in. As he lay down on his wet coat, he thought dismally about his first night in the trenches:

> Here I was in this horrible clay cavity, somewhere in Belgium, miles and miles from home, cold, wet through and covered with mud. Nothing could be heard except the occasional crack of the sniper's shot. In the narrow space beside me lay my equipment: my revolver and a sodden packet of cigarettes. Everything was cold, dark and damp. As far as I could see the future contained nothing but the same thing or worse ...

Bruce couldn't have known how right he was. After a short, uncomfortable doze he was woken by shouts and struck his head on the dugout ceiling as he sat up.

'We're bein' flooded out, sir,' the sergeant yelled. 'The water's a foot deep!'

As Bruce looked round, he realized he had been lying in a deepening pool and his clothes were soaked. The rest of the night was spent bailing out and vainly trying to dam the flood. The dismal work was lit by the menacing glare of German **star shells**.

Billets
Trench life, like the first glutinous night spent by Bruce,

was so hard and dismal that troops soon became exhausted. Another officer in Belgium, Major Bonham-Carter, wrote:

> The continual standing on wet ground, the wearing of wet boots for several days without a change and of wet clothes have a very bad effect on the men, who in some cases can barely move when they leave the trenches.

To keep soldiers fighting fit, a tour of duty in the front lines was rewarded with a few days in support lines – 'in rest'. They would leave grey with weariness and caked in dirt, but with every step towards **billets** and a break their mood improved. Unbroken sleep, a hot bath, clean clothes and a decent meal did wonders for soldiers' spirits. Wages, a bob a day (5p) for an ordinary infantryman, were paid on the first day out of line. The money was soon spent, however, on cigarettes, women and cheap white wine.

Bruce remembered other simpler pleasures too: 'One could walk about the fields nearby, could read, write letters and sleep as much as one liked.' You can guess then that he was not exactly delighted to hear that his battalion was due back in the Plugstreet trenches for Christmas. 'So that's the festivities knocked on the head,' he moaned. What he could not have known was that Christmas 1914 was to be one of the strangest days of the war.

Christmas Eve

As the Warwickshires 'went in' again on 23 December, a small miracle improved their mood – it stopped raining. The weather became fine and cold. When Bruce woke on the morning of Christmas Eve he looked out on a scene that was almost beautiful. The frozen swamp of mud between the lines glistened with frost in the sun. There was even a fine sprinkling of snow in places.

The spirit of peace seemed to infect both armies. There was no shelling and little rifle fire. Plans were made for parties in the British dugouts and Bruce spent the evening at a special trench dinner for officers – there was a bottle of red wine and 'a medley of tinned things from home' to go with the usual **bully beef**. About 22:00 he was back in his own dugout when the sound of a German band and singing drifted over.

'Do you hear the **Boches** kicking up that racket over there?' Bruce quipped to his platoon commander.

'Yes, they've been at it some time.'

'Come on, let's go along the trench to the hedge there on the right – that's the nearest point to them, over there.'

As the two men moved closer they could hear the band scratching out a version of '**Deutschland, Deutschland über Alles**'. British 'mouth organ experts' hit back with ragtime songs and a copy of the German tune.

Suddenly Bruce heard a shout, 'Come over here', in a strong German accent.

This was met by rude blasts from mouth organs and mocking laughter. Then, after a short lull, a British sergeant yelled, 'Come over here.'

'You come halfway, I come halfway,' the German replied.

'Come on then!' shouted the sergeant. 'I'm coming along the hedge.'

'Ah, but there are two of you.'

At last one wary British sergeant and one cautious German moved slowly and suspiciously towards each other. Both had the same fears.

Was it a trap?

Could the Tommy/**Hun** be trusted to come alone?

In sight now.

Careful. Watch him.

Only a few yards.

They met.

As Bruce and the other Warwickshires listened, they could hear a smattering of conversation taking place out there in the darkness. Then the sergeant came back. He gleefully showed off the cigars and cigarettes he'd swapped for a tin of Capstan tobacco. He was safe. Bruce recalled: 'It had given just the requisite touch to our Christmas Eve, something a little human and out of the ordinary routine.' But there was more to come.

Christmas Day

Most people have a fantasy Christmas present in mind.

When he stirred on Christmas morning Bruce imagined a big one:

> I should like to have suddenly heard an immense siren blowing; everybody to stop and say, 'What was that?' Siren blowing again; appearance of a small figure running across the frozen mud waving something. He gets closer – a telegraph boy with a wire! He hands it to me. With trembling fingers I open it: 'War off, return home – George R.I.' [the King]

The reality wasn't too bad though. The morning was fine and crisp. The cratered turnip field looked its best ... and the Germans were up to something! As he looked out of his trench, Bruce saw a lot of unusual activity:

> Heads were bobbing about and showing over their parapet in a most reckless way ... A complete Boche figure suddenly appeared and looked about itself. This complaint became infectious. It didn't take 'Our Bert' long to be up on the skyline (it is one long grind to ever keep him off it). This was the signal for more Boche anatomy to be disclosed and this was replied to by all our Alfs and Bills until, in less time than it takes to tell, half a dozen or so each of the **belligerents** were outside their trenches and advancing towards each other in no man's land. A strange sight, truly.

After a minute Bruce joined his wayward men. Dressed in a muddy khaki suit, a green sheepskin coat and a balaclava helmet, he sauntered towards German lines. It was so confusing, especially for an officer of the British Army. Here were the enemy they were all supposed to hate, capering about in the open. He couldn't help his nit-picking first impressions:

> The difference in type between our men and theirs was very marked. Our men in their costumes of dirty khaki with headdresses of woollen hats and mufflers were light-hearted, open and humorous as opposed to the sombre demeanour and stolid appearance of the Huns in their grey-green faded uniforms, top boots and pork-pie hats.

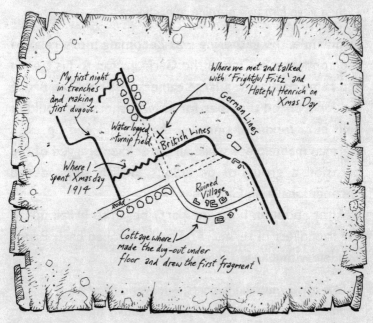

Map of the truce

Yet as the troops mingled in the middle of the turnip field, Bruce's feelings changed. **Fritz** was human too. Curious German soldiers inspected him and asked, '*Offizier?*' He nodded in reply. Everyone started to talk, smile . . . and laugh. There was fervent souvenir hunting.

Bruce chatted to a German lieutenant and, 'being a bit of a collector', pointed to their buttons.

> *We both said things to each other which neither*
> *understood, and agreed to a swap. I brought out my*
> *wire clippers and with a few deft snips removed a*
> *couple of his buttons and put them in my pocket. I*
> *then gave him two of mine in exchange.*

Meanwhile, the gathering was becoming more relaxed and comfortable. One of the Germans ran to his trench and came back with a large camera. The soldiers, Bruce included, posed together for several shots. He couldn't help but wonder if one day they would end up on a German mantelpiece while an old soldier bragged of the occasion a group of perfidious English surrendered unconditionally on Christmas Day.

After about an hour the party began to break up on the friendliest of terms. And, as he strolled back, Bruce was left with a lingering image:

> *One of my machine gunners, who was a bit of an*
> *amateur hairdresser in civil life, was cutting the*
> *unnaturally long hair of a docile Boche, who was*

patiently kneeling on the ground whilst the automatic
clippers crept up the back of his neck.

The Christmas mood lingered for a while. The Warwickshires stayed in the lines for another two days and there was no fighting. Bruce was able to indulge his collecting habit again too. He'd had his eye on a German rifle that had been lying near a couple of corpses for almost a month. Any earlier attempt to bag it would have been fatal, but now he simply walked over, picked it up and returned without any trouble. For his men, there was more singing and the treat of night-time fires without the risk of a sniper's bullet.

But the generals on both sides were furious as news of the Christmas truce spread. What on earth was going on? And how dangerous was it? Would the men start to disobey orders too?

The Warwickshires and other unwarlike units on both sides were ordered out of the line. For their replacements it was business as usual.

FIGHTING FACTS

A Cartoon War

In January 1915 life on the front line looked up for Bruce. He and a squad of men were detailed to defend the ruined village of St Yvon. Among the battered houses there was one that was a little less damaged by shellfire. This was to become his 'home' for two months. Mercifully, it was dry and free from mud, but with a roof came other problems. No one dared to move during the day in case the sharp-eyed Germans realized that the ruins were occupied and

"Well, If you knows of a better 'ole, Go to it."

Bruce Bairnsfather became one of the most popular cartoonists of the war among the troops, because he conveyed their point of view

started pounding the village again. Faced with hours of enforced idleness, he took up an old hobby and began to draw cartoons.

Bruce sketched on scraps of paper, wooden ration boxes, the crumbling plaster walls of the cottage – in fact, on any clean, dry surface. His subjects were the men around him and the miserable surroundings they lived in, but were always drawn with humour and a joke. His work became so popular that visitors helped themselves to favourite scenes and took them to decorate their grimy dugouts. Encouraged by this, he sent his first cartoon, 'Where did that one go to?' to the *Bystander* magazine. It was accepted and his career as a cartoonist began.

The Trench Experience

In 2002 the BBC showed a TV programme called *The Trench*. A group of modern volunteers re-created the

British troops leave the safety of their trench to go 'over the top'

lives of World War I soldiers, living in the open — whatever the weather.

Bruce would have been fascinated. He had already thought of the idea and in 1916 wrote his own 'tongue in cheek' instructions for anyone in England curious enough to want to share the 'trench experience':

> I recommend the following procedure. Select a flat ten-acre ploughed field, so sited that all the surface water of the surrounding country drains into it. Now cut a zigzag slot four feet deep and three wide diagonally across, dam off as much water as you can so as to leave about 100 yards of squelchy mud, delve out a hole at one side of the slot then try to live there for a month on bully beef and biscuits, whilst a friend has instructions to fire at you with his Winchester (rifle) every time you put your head above the surface.

Football Fun

Many British and German troops were ardent football fans and there are several reports that ordinary soldiers carried footballs in their knapsacks, always eager for a 'kickabout'. Captain J. L. Jack of the Scottish Rifles wrote of his own men: 'However tired the rascals may be for parades, they always have enough energy for football.'

It was hardly surprising, then, that organizing a game against the enemy soon sprang to mind during the Christmas Truce. Of course, there were problems. In many areas no man's land was a muddy, pulverized and frozen mess. Nevertheless, plans were made.

Private William Trapp of the Warwickshires, based near Plugstreet Wood, noted: 'We are trying to arrange a football match with them [a German unit from Saxony] for tomorrow, Boxing Day.' To his annoyance British artillery fire put an end to the scheme. But others were more successful. One of the best stories was told by an old soldier, Ernie Williams, in a TV interview in 1983. He was serving in the 6th Cheshires near Wulverghem in Belgium:

> *The ball appeared from somewhere, I don't know where, but it came from their side. They made up some goals and one fellow went in goal and then it was just a general kickabout. I should think there were about a couple of hundred taking part. I had a go at the ball. I was pretty good then, at nineteen. Everybody seemed to be enjoying themselves. There was no referee and no score, no tally at all ... Those great big boots [army boots] we had on were a menace – and in those days the balls were made of leather and they soon got very soggy.*

Christmas Treats

Every British soldier, and the 1,500 nurses serving alongside them, was sent a Christmas present in the name of King George V's daughter, 17-year-old Princess Mary. The small brass box held cigarettes, a pipe and pipe tobacco, a photograph of the Princess and a Christmas card greeting in the King's handwriting: 'May God protect you and bring you home safe.' For non-smokers there was a tin of sweets and some writing paper and for nurses, chocolates and a card. Over 400,000 royal presents were shipped out and delivered by 25 December. There were so many that complaints were received because they were filling up the supply trains to the front – and ammunition was being left behind!

Truce Tales

The Christmas Truce didn't stop fighting along the whole of the Western Front, but troops in many areas did cease fire for a while. And there were reports of heart-warming incidents on all sides.

Carol Competition

Graham Williams of the London Rifle Brigade remembered an unusual carol concert:

> They finished their carol so we thought we ought to retaliate, so we sang 'The First Noel', and when we finished that they all began clapping: and they struck up another favourite of theirs, 'O Tannenbaum'. And so it went on ... when we started 'O Come, All Ye Faithful' the Germans immediately joined in, singing the same hymn to the words 'Adeste, Fideles'. And I thought this is a really extraordinary thing – two nations singing the same carol in the middle of a war.

Operatic War

The German Crown Prince Wilhelm, son of the Kaiser, decided to visit his troops on Christmas Eve. He was Commander of the German Fifth Army, stationed in the Argonne region of France. As he moved forward there was the usual grim face of war: the howl of shells, bursts of machine-gun fire and the crump of trench mortars. Yet Wilhelm recalled, 'Every dugout had its Christmas tree, and from all directions came the sound of rough men's voices singing our exquisite old songs.'

And if it was songs the soldiers wanted, they were in for a wonderful surprise. The Prince had brought a star from the Berlin Opera with him, Walter Kirchoff, the tenor. While Wilhelm handed out Iron Crosses (medals) in the safety of the reserve trenches, Kirchoff went up to the front line to perform. The next day he told the Prince that 'some French soldiers had climbed up on to the **parapet** to applaud, until at last he gave them an encore'.

Just Like Diwali

Thousands of Indian troops served alongside the British and saw heavy fighting. The Garhwal Rifles, dug in near the village of Neuve-Chapel, were having a miserable time. Their trenches were a little downhill from those of the enemy and when the Germans pumped the water from their lines it flowed straight into those of the unlucky Garhwalis.

But on Christmas Eve the normally fierce Germans began behaving strangely. The Indians could hear them singing carols and watched in astonishment as they placed small candle-lit trees in rows along their parapets. The candles struck a chord with the Garhwalis. During the Hindu festival of Diwali, celebrated each autumn, earthenware oil lamps are lit in the evening and set up in rows outside temples and houses. In the middle of a European winter it was a reminder of home.

Wotcha, Cock. How's London?

Graham Williams of the London Rifles enjoyed the truce more than most. He was a fluent German speaker and in great demand on Christmas morning. He was having a good chinwag with a group of Germans in no man's land when one piped up in a broad cockney accent, 'Wotcha, Cock. How's London?'

Taken aback, Graham replied, 'Good Lord, you speak like a Londoner.'

German: 'Well, I am a Londoner!'

Graham: 'Well, what on earth are you doing in the German army?'

German: 'I'm a German – a German Londoner.'

Graham recalled:

Apparently he had been born in Germany, but had gone to London as a baby with his parents, who had a small business in the East End somewhere. He'd been

*brought up in England and gone to school in England.
But by German law he was still a German national –
he'd never been naturalized [become a British citizen]
– he had been called up to Germany to do his national
service: they did three years at that time. And
afterwards he came back to London, joined his parents
and got a job as a porter at Victoria station.*

Old Joe Whip

Sing to the tune of the chorus of 'Casey Jones'

Old Joe Whip, mounted on the parapet
Old Joe Whip, a **Mills bomb** in his hand,
Old Joe Whip, he stopped a blooming **whizzbang**
Now he's a bomber in the promised land.

Trench song

AN UNDERGROUND WAR

BATTLE BRIEFING

The Ypres Salient

During the autumn of 1914 the British army held little more than 20 miles (32 km) of trenches on the Western Front. The key to this sector was the ancient cloth-making town of Ypres and the ground held in front of it – the grim Ypres **salient**. This formed a bulge in the British line that stuck out for 3 miles (5 km), like a crooked nose on a face (see map). And like a nose, it was just as vulnerable in a fight.

Still hopeful of a quick victory, the Germans launched a ferocious attack to break through to the sea on 20 October – the first Battle of Ypres. The British were outnumbered two to one in men and five to one in artillery, but managed to hang on. On one appalling day, the astonished Tommies watched as thousands of soldiers in long grey lines advanced towards

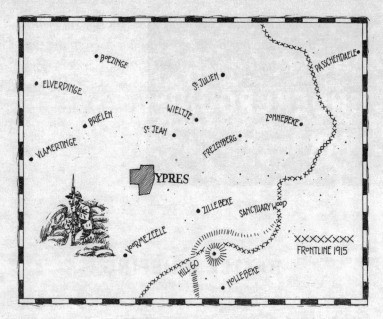

Map of the area surrounding Ypres

them, arms locked together and singing. They were student volunteers, thrown into battle with only six weeks' training. British artillery and machine guns ripped the lines to pieces. In three weeks 36,000 students died, a loss the Germans still call the Kindermord – the Massacre of the Children.

Although beaten back, the Germans made some key gains during November. They dug in on the Messines Ridge, a 15-mile (24-km) spine of higher ground that partly encircled Ypres. And, crucially, they captured the highest point of the ridge – Hill 60.

Yet to call it a hill was an absurdity. Hill 60 was a man-made mound, built with the spoil from a nearby railway cutting. So called because it was only 200 feet (60 m) high, it was nevertheless the hinge of the German line. From the top, artillery spotters had a clear view over the flat Flanders Plain, especially of Ypres and the exposed salient. No sooner had the German attacks stopped than the British schemed to retake it.

Panoramic view of Hill 60, near Ypres, 10 April 1915

Infantry assaults soon became fruitless slaughters and early in 1915 the generals realized it was time to try something different. Something the Germans had already used with stunning results – mining. Now it was time to strike back … and the target was Hill 60.

TUNNELLING TERRORS

Indian Nightmare
Indian troops had been holding 10 miles (16 km) of the British line, near Festubert, since November 1914. But they were uneasy. Many were worn out by hard fighting and the miserable weather of a European winter. And

31

then there were the rumours. Some men swore they had heard muffled banging, others the cushioned sound of digging. A few had been told that pilots in the Royal Flying Corps had seen mounds of discoloured soil behind enemy lines. Could it be that the Germans were digging mines under their feet? Or was this simply more idle trench gossip?

On 19 December torrential rain fell endlessly and there was no time for tittle-tattle. Trenches flooded, **fire steps** were washed away and, despite the soldiers' best efforts, their rifles often clogged with mud and jammed. At dawn on 20 December heavy German artillery and mortar fire seared the whole of the sector. Enemy attacks punched in near Givenchy and were hurled back only after bitter **skirmishes**.

Then, at 09:00, three mysterious flares arced into the air over the German trenches. Moments later 10 terrific explosions rocked the line held by the Sirhind Brigade. The ground shook and split. Tons of earth, together with men and weapons, were tossed 20 feet (6 m) in the air. The rumours were true. The Germans had tunnelled under the Indian trenches and fired powerful mines. Everyone close by was killed, while anyone within 160 feet (50 m) was knocked out or too dazed to fight on.

Waves of German assault troops dashed across no man's land and stormed the Indian lines. In the dugouts they found the bodies of dozens of men sitting as if they were asleep – killed by the explosions. Reinforcements were rushed in, but it was not until 22 December that the enemy was driven off. The first underground attack of the war had been stunningly successful.

Clay-kickers

In England one man was already working hard to hit back. Norton Griffiths was the Member of Parliament for Wednesbury in the West Midlands and the wealthy owner of a contracting business. He had made his fortune building railways and running mining operations around the world. A larger-than-life character, he was tall, handsome and outrageously confident. No sooner had the fighting begun than he turned his immense energy to helping the war effort. And he reckoned he had just the idea the army needed: clay-kicking!

In Britain Griffiths and Company had won the contract to build the Manchester sewerage system. Miles of underground tunnels were being driven through the clay subsoil by a group of elite miners using an unusual technique. They sat with their backs supported by a wooden framework and kicked their spades into the clay. The spoil was then passed back to a mate for removal. Proudly, the Manchester workers nicknamed themselves 'Moles' and their method 'clay-kicking'. In the right conditions they were the best miners in the world. Just the men needed, thought Norton, for digging tunnels under the enemy's trenches.

For weeks he badgered the War Office with a scheme

to take a force of Moles to France, but his pleas were ignored until the success of German mining operations. By February 1915 the enemy had exploded more mines and British troops had come to dread these underground explosions more than machine-gun fire or the crash of shells. Protests poured in from frontline officers. Something must be done, they demanded, or morale would collapse.

At last, on 14 February, Norton was summoned to see Field Marshal Kitchener, the Secretary of State for War, and given a chance to explain his ideas. In a dramatic pantomime, he snatched the coal shovel from the fireplace, sat on the floor and clay-kicked for his one-man audience. Kitchener was entranced and ordered him to go to France to consult with the top officers in the Royal Engineers (the army's own force of builders and engineers). This time, Norton found himself banging on an open door. The Royal Engineers welcomed his input and agreed there was an urgent need for expert mining units. By 19 February the War Office agreed to form the first eight tunnelling companies as soon as possible.

Norton flung his energy into finding recruits. Among the first were 18 of his Manchester clay-kickers. Before long, they were joined by miners of every type from across the country, including Scottish coal miners, Welsh slate miners and Cornish tin miners. And an unattractive lot they looked to army eyes – many were unusually small, others middle-aged and more than a few in their sixties, with white hair and missing teeth. They didn't take kindly to army discipline and were known to argue openly with their officers. One compensation was the pay – 6s 6d a day (32.5p), far higher than ordinary soldiers earned and better than most were paid in their civilian jobs. Norton added his own exciting spin to those he met personally: 'When the plunger's pressed, boys,' he said, grinning, 'you'll have a front-seat view of the Germans going up.'

Other men with mining experience were already in the army. They had joined up when the war began and now the call went out for them to transfer to the tunnelling companies.

One volunteer was Private Garfield Morgan of the South Wales Borderers. His career began with a rebellion. Twelve ex-miners from the Borderers were sent to London to be interviewed by Norton. On the way they were given a warning by the friendly sergeant-major who escorted them: 'Watch out. He might try to sign you up for 2s 2d [12.5p]. That's standard **sapper** pay. Stick out for the higher rate.'

One by one they filed in to see Norton, were offered 2s 2d and, to his fury, turned it down.

'Get out!' he yelled to each.

Forlornly, they prepared to march away when a booming voice called out, 'Halt the men, Sergeant-Major. Send them back.'

It was Norton. The soldiers had him over a barrel and he knew it. Stifling his anger, he offered them the top rate and, to show there were no hard feelings, threw in an extra 1s 9d (9p) ration money for that day's food.

Hill 60

As the new tunnelling units were hurried across the Channel in late February, the army was already preparing a nasty surprise for them. Their first target had been chosen, the sinister Hill 60. On 8 March work began on three tunnels: M1, M2 and M3. Garfield Morgan was put to work on M3, with a starting point just behind British lines and only 150 feet (45 m) from the German trenches. The first day wasn't good. As Garfield and his

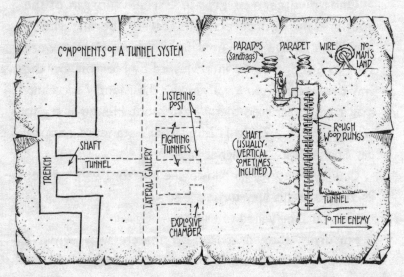

Plan of a tunnel

mate Albert Rees started work on the shaft, they uncovered the rotting body of a French soldier. In the next two hours they exposed three more corpses and, trying desperately not to be sick, tipped them into body bags. After dark they dragged them back for burial in a grave lined with **quicklime**.

Working round the clock in eight-hour shifts, the miners drove the tunnels forward 10 feet (3 m) a day. The thick Flanders clay was perfect for 'clay-kicking', but if the digging was trouble-free, other perils lay in wait. Although the tunnels were lined with stout timber boards, liquid mud burst through the joints in powerful jets. Worse, ventilation rapidly became a problem. When the air turned fetid, the only air pumps available were left over from the Crimean War – 60 years earlier! These noisy antiques were almost useless and had to be replaced with a hastily rigged system. Large bellows, like those in a blacksmith's shop, were used to blow fresh air down a hosepipe to the men hacking at the clay.

But the flow was never enough. Candles would grow dim and splutter out, while matches glowed a strange cherry red without bursting into flame. Lack of oxygen gave the miners blinding headaches and their chests heaved and wheezed in an eerie roaring noise. Many were dragged to the surface blue and gasping for breath long before their shifts had finished. In M3 Garfield sustained lasting damage to his eyes.

All the work had to be done in near silence to avoid

discovery. The miners talked in whispers, while tools were used gently and iron parts muffled in cloth. Even so, the Germans suspected something was up. Listening posts tried to detect the noise of the British excavations, while enemy engineers set off explosives to shake the tunnels down. Every day the miners faced the risk of being killed by concussion or by being buried alive in a tomb of their own making.

In early April Garfield and Albert were working at the face of M3a (a branch of M3) when Albert felt his shovel break through into ... nothing. With his spade waggling in thin air, he called Garfield over to look at the ragged black hole on the left-hand side of the tunnel. Turning quickly, he snuffed out the candle just in time to hear footsteps splash by on the other side of the cavity. It was a German tunnel! Shocked, they scrambled back to find an officer.

An hour later they were back with Second Lieutenant Thomas Black. In pitch darkness the three men slowly edged along the tunnel until they came to the hole. No sooner had Thomas switched on his electric torch, than ... CRACK ... a bullet ripped through the sleeve of his uniform. This sent them clawing their way back along M3 to the safety of the shaft entrance, their ears ringing from the boom of the gun firing in such a cramped space. When the miners plucked up courage to return a second time they found a canister of German explosives wired to fire. They cut the leads and replaced the enemy

German miners

device with their own huge charges of **guncotton**. But what would happen next? With M3 and M3a discovered, the success of the attack rested on the two other tunnels.

Boom Time
By Saturday 10 April the digging at Hill 60 was almost finished. M1 and M2 extended 300 feet (90 m) beneath

no man's land, before splaying out into four smaller branches under enemy lines. Now the last and most dangerous job lay ahead: bringing up the explosives. Major David Griffiths, the officer in charge of the operation, calculated he needed 4 tons of gunpowder to blow up Hill 60. That meant over 90 bags of powder, each weighing 100 lb (45 kg) to be carried from the rear trenches by hand.

The miners worked in teams of three to lug their deadly loads – two men to lift a bag on to the shoulders of the third, with a stop every 300 feet to change over. Night after night they risked the terrifying journey, slipping and sliding on muddy duckboards. Only black humour relieved the screaming ache of their muscles – just how many pieces would they be blown into if a stray shell landed nearby?

At last the gunpowder was winched down the shafts and hauled to the end of the tunnels. Behind the charges sandbag walls were built 10 feet (3 m) thick to make sure the blast went upwards towards the enemy. In case of problems, two fuses were laid to waterproof the ignition charges in each tunnel – simple burning fuses and high-tech electrical wires running back to plungers. By 15 April everything was ready for zero hour.

The last 48 hours were a nightmare of waiting. Every inch of fuse was checked every two hours in case of breaks, the miners crawling in the dark with their flashlights. Alarmingly, German digging could be heard above M1 and M2. It was clear the enemy now had their own tunnels and a race was on. Were they almost ready to blow their mines too? No one could be sure.

After a long winter, 17 April was a fine spring day. There was sunshine and a warm breeze. As evening drew on, the shelling subsided, as if both sides were settling down for a pleasant rest. In the unusual quiet, the British mines were detonated at 19:05.

The explosion lasted for 10 long seconds. Hill 60 burst open like a volcano, and debris was flung 300 feet into the air. Mud, sandbags and bodies rained down. The shockwaves left the German survivors dazed and helpless. A British artillery bombardment began at once and the infantry went over the top. In less than 15 minutes the battered remains of Hill 60 were in British hands.

FIGHTING FACTS

Holding On

The course of war is rarely clear and the British soon discovered that taking Hill 60 was the easy part. Keeping it became a nightmare. The hill and the shattered ground around it were a tiny wedge – only 750 feet (230 m) long and 600 feet (180 m) wide – poking into German lines. It was exposed to enemy fire from two sides and by 20:00 that same evening accurate German gunners were already pounding the site. During that first night there were four ferocious counter-attacks – and the enemy kept coming. Over the next three days four Victoria Crosses (medals) were won by courageous soldiers as the British clung on desperately to a killing field. After the war one historian called Hill 60 'a rubbish heap in which it is impossible to dig without disturbing a body'.

Gas

The first British infantry on Hill 60 sent back a series of alarming reports. Some men had collapsed, gasping for breath, convinced they had been gassed. And they were right – they had been gassed by accident! The Germans had been planning an attack with this frightening new weapon and were positioning cylinders of chlorine when the British fired their mines. Some of the cylinders had cracked and the gas leaked slowly out. Unfortunately, in the heat of battle, the reports were ignored. It seemed more likely to the authorities that the men had been affected by fumes from bursting shells or from the gunpowder in the mines. A vital warning had been missed.

On 22 April 1915 the Germans launched the first gas attack on the Western Front, against French troops holding the line north of Ypres. Newly arrived Algerians were the first to breathe the deadly fumes and fell back in panic, choking and vomiting.

At 08:45 on 4 May the exhausted defenders on Hill

60 spotted a dense bluish cloud drifting towards them. With only cotton pads to press to their faces, there was little they could do. Shortly after the gas swirled into the British trenches a fierce German assault retook the broken hill. One victim was Garfield Morgan, who staggered back towards Ypres, clutching his throat and throwing up bright green vomit. It took him 11 weeks in hospital to recover.

Messines Ridge

In June 1917 the British began the third Battle of Ypres — one more attempt to break through the German lines in Belgium. What made this attack unique was the use of mines of unimaginable power. Nineteen tunnels were dug altogether, a total length of $4^{1}/_{2}$ miles (7 km), and charged with 500 tons of explosive.

The tunnelling had started 18 months earlier and was finished a year before the assault. The work was carried out in the strictest secrecy and silence. Lieutenant Bryan Frayling of 171 Tunnelling Company remembered: 'We wore felt slippers, used rubber-wheeled trolleys on wooden rails and spoke in whispers.'

Even so, the enemy was active, listening for the British and digging their own counter-tunnels. Sometimes, when German workings were detected, a small mine would be fired to destroy them — hopefully without damaging the British tunnels too much. And of course the Germans were trying to do exactly the same. It was a tense battle of wits and timing, with the miners never knowing if they were about to be buried alive. And sometimes, if a tunnel was vital, the British weren't allowed to hit first. Lieutenant Frayling commented:

> The Germans were down below and every now and again gave us trouble. When the Germans 'blew' us we never answered back, we suffered casualties and did nothing, tried not to give away where we were. We listened for them with very delicate instruments, like the geophone. One of our officers was once so near to a German shaft that he wrote down and translated a series of yarns that the German NCO told his shift.

Finally, at 03:10 on 7 June, the mines were fired – 17 detonating simultaneously. The noise, a drawn-out roar, was heard hundreds of miles away. A captain in the Royal Engineers wrote:

> It seemed as if the Messines Ridge got up and shook itself. All along its flank belched rows of mushroom-shaped masses of debris, flung high in the air. Gradually the masses commenced to disintegrate, as the released gases forced their way through the centres in pillars of flames. Then along the enemy line rolled dense columns of smoke, tumbling into weird formations as they mounted into the sky.

More horribly, Lieutenant Frayling noted:

The flames went up higher than St Paul's. I estimated about 800 feet. It was a white incandescent light, we knew that the temperature was about 3,000 degrees centigrade. The Germans there went up as gas. The biggest bit of a German I found afterwards was one foot in a boot.

German resistance on the ridge collapsed and by 05:00 it was in British hands. Over 7,000 prisoners were taken, together with 48 guns and 218 machine guns. The assault was a rare success. Unfortunately, the main attack went ahead three weeks later and became bogged down in

The ruins of Ypres, 22 November 1916. This battered city came to symbolize the plight of the Belgian people

frightful weather around the village of Passchendaele –
the name by which the battle became better known.
More than 300,000 British and Empire troops were
killed or injured.

Missing Mine

Only 17 mines were detonated on 7 June 1917? Yes,
you're right – two were missing! One was discovered in
1955 and blown up. The other is still down there . . .
deadly and undiscovered.

Hanging on the Old Barbed Wire

If you want to find the old battalion,
I know where they are, I know where they are,
I know where they are.
If you want to find the old battalion,
I know where they are.
They're hanging on the old barbed wire.
I've seen 'em, I've seen 'em,
Hanging on the old barbed wire.
I've seen 'em, I've seen 'em,
Hanging on the old barbed wire.

Trench song

GALLIPOLI – A SIDE SHOW

BATTLE BRIEFING

The Lure of Constantinople

By 1915 it was clear that victory on the Western Front would be hard won. There had already been nearly a million Allied casualties. Horrified by the killing match in France, powerful voices in the British government began to look round for easier options. 'Why,' they argued, 'hammer at the front door of the enemy if we can sneak up from behind?'

Winston Churchill, the First Lord of the Admiralty, had his own pet scheme: to pick off one of Germany's newest allies, Turkey. And he believed he was in charge of just the service to do this quickly and cheaply: the Royal Navy. Churchill proposed that a fleet of battleships should smash through Turkish defences on the straits of the Dardanelles and threaten Constantinople (today known as Istanbul). This, he argued, would bring a host of advantages to the Allies.

Turkey and Gallipoli peninsula, 1915

War-winning Advantage 1

The Turkish government, which supported Germany, would be thrown out and replaced by Turks who would back the Allies.

War-winning Advantage 2

Other countries in the area, such as Greece and Bulgaria, would look to the Allies for leadership and threaten Austria-Hungary, Germany's partner.

War-winning Advantage 3

Hard-pressed Russia would be able to export grain through

the Black Sea and earn money to pay for her armies on the Eastern Front.

You can see the geographical importance of Turkey from the map on page 49. No wonder breaching the Dardanelles seemed like a magical solution to the war!

A Gamble on the Fleet

And it almost came off. By February 1915 the strongest fleet ever seen in the Mediterranean was stationed off the straits. A British officer wrote: 'It looked as if no human power could withstand such an array of might.' In softening-up operations, Turkish forts were shelled and anti-ship mines cleared until the British admiral, de Roebuck, judged the time was right to attack.

On 18 March, a hot spring morning, a combined force of 18 British and French battleships, guarded by an armada of cruisers and destroyers, began to fight their way through. Several ships were hit, but they suffered little damage and by 14:00 the Allies were almost 10 miles (16 km) into enemy waters and going well. The bombardment had shaken the Turks and their official version of the action states:

> All telephone wires were cut, all communications with
> the forts were interrupted, some guns had been
> knocked out and others half buried, others again were
> out of action with the breech mechanism jammed.

Then abruptly the tide of battle turned. The French

battleship Bouvet *hit a mine and vanished in less than a minute, with the loss of almost 600 men. By 18:00 two more battleships had been sunk by mines and three seriously damaged. Shaken by losing a third of his force, de Roebuck pulled out. In the coming days he glumly decided that the Dardanelles could not be cracked open by ships alone. Troops had to land on the Gallipoli peninsula and knock out the enemy guns. Little did he know that by nightfall on 18 March, the Turks were almost out of ammunition. One more push would have seen his fleet within firing range of Constantinople.*

The Army Steps In

The very idea that troops might be needed to support the navy caused weeks of fierce argument in the British government. It wasn't until mid-March that Field Marshal Kitchener, the Secretary of State for War, agreed. After that everything happened in a messy rush. Sir Ian Hamilton was given command of the Mediterranean Expeditionary Force (MEF) to Gallipoli, but left England with almost no idea of what he faced. He had no detailed maps, no information about the enemy and no battle plan.

Sir Ian took his first look at the Gallipoli peninsula from the deck of the battleship Queen Elizabeth – and he was daunted. The terrain was bleak, a gnarled finger of hilly land 50 miles (80 km) long, riven by steep ravines. He reported to Kitchener, 'It looks a much tougher nut to crack than it did over the map in your office.'

This was the understatement of the year! From the start, Gallipoli was a ramshackle campaign and this woeful situation was to cost thousands of lives ...

V BEACH

Making Do

To crack open Gallipoli, Sir Ian was given a force of 75,000 troops, largely the British 29th Division and the Anzacs (the Australian and New Zealand Army Corps). The troops trained briefly in Egypt before moving to the Greek island of Lemnos for the final attack. Sir Ian made his plans at breakneck speed but surprise was the last thing he could hope for. Every move the MEF made was watched by Turkish spies and reported to Constantinople.

Sir Ian was well aware that his men faced the toughest of jobs – landing from the sea against an enemy dug in and waiting – and yet they had arrived without the most basic supplies. His list of urgent worries ran like this:

- My men don't have enough ammunition.
- They have no grenades.
- They only have a handful of mortars.
- Worst of all, there are no landing craft to get them ashore!

*

To Sir Ian's fury, the landing craft were ready and waiting, but in England. There was a small fleet of armoured barges, built for an **amphibious attack** in the Baltic – an attack that never happened. However, when he asked for them he was curtly refused. Instead, MEF officers had to scour Egypt to buy every spare tug and small boat for the landings, every donkey for transport, and every skin, and every oil drum and kerosene tin to hold water.

Sir Ian threw his efforts into the landing plans. How and where, he pondered, would he get enough men ashore to set up a **bridgehead**? And how would he trick the Turks so they didn't wipe out his men on the beaches? By mid-April the details were ready.

The British Plan

The main assault force, the 29th Division, would punch inland from three tiny beaches at the tip of Cape Hellas. They were codenamed X, W and V. The landing commander was to be General Hunter-Watson.

To divide and confuse the Turks, 2,000 men would hit Y beach further north (see map on page 54), while the Anzacs would storm ashore at Gaba Tepe, Z beach.

Sir Ian was convinced that once the British were on land the enemy would crumble. And his men agreed. An Australian private summed up the cocky mood of the army when he wrote home: 'Who could stop us? Not the bloody Turks!'

53

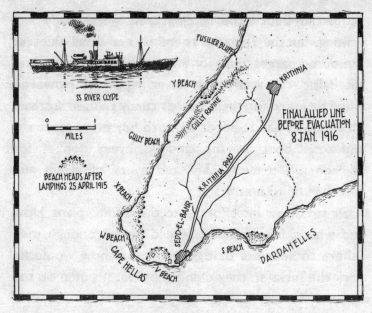

British landings at V beach

The final date set for the landings was 25 April, only a few weeks since Sir Ian had been given the job. Amazingly fast. But not fast enough.

Tough Turkey

Like a team briefing before a football match, the British had studied the form of the Turks — and didn't rate them. They would soon crumble, like the native armies thrashed in dozens of wars across the Empire. And a close look at a Turkish unit would have done nothing to change this opinion. Many soldiers wore tattered uniforms, with shoes made from rags and tied together with string. But this opinion was a big mistake.

As far as the Turks were concerned, they had just given the greatest navy in the world a bloody nose. And they were ready to hand out more punishment. The German general Otto Liman von Sanders was given command of the defences on the Gallipoli peninsula and worked his own miracle.

The Turkish Defence

Troops scattered thinly round the entire coastline were pulled back to form mobile reserves.

At the same time the defences around every possible landing site were strengthened with new, deep trenches and barbed wire.

Liman von Sanders gleefully wrote: 'The British allowed us four weeks of respite for all this good work before their great disembarkation [landing] . . . this was just enough.'

With every day that passed the Gallipoli nut got tougher.

Robert Unwin's Brainwave

The British knew that the success of the operation depended on landing plenty of men fast and swamping the Turks. But without landing craft what could be done? The navy came up with a plan. Warships would transport the troops to within a mile of the beaches and then ferry them ashore in strings of small boats called 'tows'.

Each tow would be hauled by a powered tug. It was risky but there was no alternative.

Thinking the problem through, Commander Robert Unwin had a brainwave. He reckoned he could go one better than the tows and use a merchant ship to land extra men in the first wave of the attack. They would go in on the key landing zone: V beach.

Robert was a seasoned Royal Navy officer and commanded the destroyer *Hussar*. Given the go-ahead, he created a secret weapon that was soon compared to the ancient Greek trick, the Trojan Horse. An innocent-looking collier (coal carrier), the *River Clyde*, was converted into an armoured landing craft. Carrying 2,000 men in her hold, she would be rammed into V beach. The troops would pour out from four large holes – or **sally ports** – cut through her steel plates and dash down gangways supported by ropes. The gangways led to a bridge made from barges lashed to the shoreline. These barges were to be towed alongside the *River Clyde* and manoeuvred into place as soon as the collier ran aground.

V Beach

The task force, over 200 ships, had gathered at Lemnos and began to move off on 23 April. By midnight on the 24th most warships, with the assault troops aboard, had reached their battle stations. Still out of sight of land, they came to a stop, and a meal of hot coffee and rolls was given to the soldiers. For many it was a last taste of luxury.

At first light, around 05:00, the assault troops got their first glimpse of V beach. It wasn't inviting. The landing zone was shaped like the sides of a bowl, with a small gravelly beach around 1,000 feet (300 m) long and 100 feet (30 m) wide. Behind this the ground rose steeply, with low cliffs on the left and a ruined fort above the village of Sedd-el-Bahr on the right. Tiers of trenches and thick rows of barbed wire ringed the beach. Unseen, but deadly, the Turks had four machine guns and two 37-mm pom-pom guns set to give a murderous crossfire.

The assault began when the battleship *Albion* opened fire to soften up the defences. For 30 minutes V beach was pounded. A little after 06:00 the *River Clyde* began her run-in, packed with 2,000 men from the Munster Fusiliers, the Dublin Fusiliers and the Hampshire Regiment. Alongside ran a tow of around 20 small boats carrying over 700 Dublins. Each man carried an 80-lb (40-kg) pack and there was little room to move. When the naval fire subsided an eerie quiet fell over the tiny bay. Surely the Turks were either dead or their morale broken? Perhaps they had taken to their heels? A staff officer on board the *River Clyde* jotted in his notebook, '6.22 a.m. Ran smoothly ashore without a tremor. No opposition. We shall land unopposed.'

But the Turks had not run away. The bombardment had barely touched their trenches or barbed-wire entanglements. They watched, waited and held their fire until the British grounded. The Dublins, in their fragile open boats, took the first deadly fusillade. Only around 300 survived the deadly machine guns to make it to the beach and many of them were wounded. Desperately, they hid behind a sand bank about 30 feet (10 m) in, helplessly pinned down. Major David French wrote:

> One of the men close to me fell dead – shot. I realized that having practically wiped out those in the three boats ahead they were now concentrating their fire on us. I jumped at once into the sea (up to my chest) yelling at the men to make a rush for it and follow me. But the poor devils – packed like sardines in a tin – could scarcely clamber over the sides and only two reached the shore un-hit. The water seemed to be alive – the bullets striking the sea all around us.

To those watching from the comparative safety of the *River Clyde* it seemed as if the Dublins were 'slaughtered like rats in a trap'. Meanwhile, the attack from the collier had its own problems.

Leaving the Clyde

When the *River Clyde* hit V beach Captain Guy Geddes, commanding a company of Munsters, noted, 'None of us felt it, there was no jar.' But there was no way off either. The steam-powered barge that was supposed to make the bridge between the ship and the shore veered to port (the left) and ran aground in the wrong place. Robert Unwin grimly realized that it was up to him to save the landing.

Shells bursting near SS *River Clyde*, V beach, Gallipoli, 1915

Since the *River Clyde* was his idea, Robert was acting as captain on the old collier that day. He left the bridge at once and dived into the sea with a rope, followed by Able Seaman William Williams. Together they lashed a couple of lighters (flat-bottomed boats for unloading ships) into position to make a causeway. But there was nothing to fasten the boats to and so no way to stop the swift current running along the coast from whipping them away. With every second vital, Robert and William decided that they would have to become living anchors to keep the boats in place.

Braced in the sea, while machine-gun bullets thrashed the water around him, Robert tied the boats to himself. A little behind, William added his weight to the line. Once secure, they yelled for the soldiers to start the landing. Gamely the men poured out of the sally ports and down the gangways – straight into the enemy guns. The massacre of the Dublins had finished minutes before and now the Turks concentrated their fire on the *River Clyde*. Soon the gangways and the causeway were choked with the dead and dying. The sea turned red with the blood of the wounded who fell overboard and drowned under the weight of their packs. Those who reached the shore dodged and slithered their way to the flimsy protection of the sandbank.

The sailors held the boats as long as they could, but soon William was hit. To stop him from drowning, Robert let go of the rope and the lighters began to move.

British troops storm ashore under heavy Turkish machine-gun fire

At just this moment Guy Geddes led his men out:

> We got it like anything, man after man behind me shot
> down, but they never wavered. Lieutenant Watts, who
> was wounded in five places and lying on the gangway,
> cheered the men on with cries of 'Follow the Captain'.
> Captain French of the Dublins told me afterwards that
> he counted the first 48 men to follow me and they all
> fell ... I stepped on to the second lighter and looked
> around to find myself alone. I jumped into the sea and
> had to swim a dozen strokes to get ashore.

By this time 51-year-old Robert was exhausted and
collapsed. He was taken back aboard the *Clyde* to recover
and his place was taken by three other brave sailors.
After less than an hour's rest he was back in the water,
holding the causeway in place again. Robert Unwin and
William Williams were awarded the Victoria Cross for
their actions. Amazingly, Robert survived the day, but
William died of his wounds shortly after he was hit.

By 09:30 over 1,000 men had charged out of the *River
Clyde*, yet more than half were killed or injured before
they reached the beach. Finally, the officers called off the
assault, now gloomily sure that nothing more could be
done until nightfall. Those left on board settled to wait
as best they could in the baking heat of the hull. They
had one comforting thought as they sweated out the
rest of the day: at least for now the steel plates of the
ship sheltered them from the enemy guns.

With good reason the Turkish commander, Colonel Mahmut, was elated. He had held the bay with only a few dozen men and proudly reported:

> The shore became full of enemy corpses, like a shoal of fish. The enemy troops were so frightened that they refused to disembark from the large transport (the River Clyde). Their officers had drawn swords and were sending men down the ladders but they were observed and could not escape our Turkish bullets.

The Second Wave

General Hunter-Watson was stationed on board the Cruiser *Euryalis*, five minutes' sailing time from V beach. But, far from knowing that the attack had collapsed, he believed all was well. At 07:50 the general was told that British troops were already in Sedd-el-Behr and moving forward. Buoyed up by this good news, he ordered the second wave, led by Brigadier General Napier, to go in at 08:30.

Impatiently Napier walked the deck of the troop transport, which in kinder days had been a cross-Channel ferry. 'Where are those damn boats? They should have returned by now,' he muttered. Then the tow came into view. Only half a dozen boats had living crews and most were packed with dead or wounded soldiers. The weary sailors said nothing. It was not their job to decide if the landing was hopeless. And Napier didn't ask their opinion.

Hastily the boats were cleared, but there were too few to carry more than the brigadier general, his staff and a few men. Nevertheless, the general was determined to get ashore and sat down carefully on the slippery, blood-soaked seats. As the tow returned to the beach at around 09:30 an astonished officer on the *River Clyde* couldn't believe his eyes. He grabbed a megaphone and called to Napier to come alongside. 'You can't possibly land,' a chorus of voices warned. But the brigadier general was made of sterner stuff. From his place in the lead boat he could see the causeway from the *River Clyde* to the shore full of men, pinned down by Turkish fire. What they needed was an example – firm leadership.

'I'll have a damned good try,' he yelled back, and sprang on board the lighters with his staff. Only then did he realize the soldiers were all dead. Seconds later, the machine guns chattered again. Napier and those with him were cut down before they could reach the beach.

FIGHTING FACTS

Bridgehead

No more men landed on V beach during daylight on 25 April but as dusk fell the remaining soldiers aboard the *River Clyde* came ashore in small parties. Second Lieutenant Gillet described the horror that met them:

A panoramic shot of the Gallipoli beachhead packed with supplies

The barges, now linked together and more or less reaching the shore, were piled high with mutilated bodies – and between the last barge and the shore was a pier formed by piles of dead men. It was impossible to reach the shore without treading on the dead, and the sea round the cove was red with blood.

Although there had been chaos at V beach, the other landings fared better and a fragile bridgehead was set up. On 26 April Turkish troops pulled back to new defences across the peninsula in front of Krithnia and the scene was set for a brutal slogging match that lasted for months. Sir Ian was relieved of command on 15 October and the new commander, General Monro, recommended

evacuation. By 9 January 1916 the British and their allies had pulled out of Gallipoli.

Fortunes of War

War is often about missed opportunities. In February 1915 the battleship *Vengeance* pounded the ancient fort at Sedd-el-Bahr and the Turkish guns were wrecked or abandoned by their crews. A party of Royal Marines and sailors landed without any trouble. They strolled up the beach to the fort and blew up undamaged guns and smashed searchlights. Satisfied with their work they left – with no sign of the Turks. As you have just read, when the British came back two months later the scene was tragically different.

Statistics from Gallipoli		
Nationality	**Casualties**	**Killed**
Australian	26,094	7,594
New Zealand	7,594	2,431
British Empire (other than Australia and New Zealand)	171,335	119,335
French	47,000	27,000
Turkish	251,309	86,000

A Dirty War

In the eight months of fierce fighting that followed the Gallipoli landings, living conditions for the British troops at Gallipoli were dirty and squalid. More men fell sick than were killed or injured in battle. Read on and shudder!

Dirty Heat

Cool weather lasted throughout May and wild flowers bloomed everywhere, even between the front lines. But by July the temperature had soared to 84 degrees Fahrenheit (29°C) in the shade – for the fortunate few who could find any shade in the arid landscape. It was so hot that the fat melted in tins of bully beef and metal plates were too hot to touch.

Dirty Water

Except for a couple of springs and some wells dug by

engineers, there was no drinking water in the Cape Hellas bridgehead. Most had to be brought in from Egypt, 700 miles (1,100 km) away, and rations were often down to 3 pints (1.8 litres) a day each for drinking and washing. Lieutenant-Colonel Burge wrote:

> The only thing there is to drink is water that comes from a well, which tastes as if it had a dead mule in it (it probably has). However, we are given purifying tablets, which are very good and make the water taste as if it had two dead mules in it.

Dirty Food

Gallipoli rations: bully beef, army biscuits, apricot or plum jam and tea without milk.

Occasional treats: rum, bread, condensed milk.

Fresh food: throw a hand grenade into the sea and collect the stunned and dead fish.

A Gallipoli Recipe:

*Take two or three hard biscuits
    (supplied by Huntley and Palmers)
Bash with entrenching tool (small shovel) till pulverized
Mix with water to make flour
Roll into ball in khaki handkerchief (preferably unused)
Boil in water in mess tin*

It was horrible but at least it was different!

Dirty Lice

Most soldiers fought three wars in Gallipoli: one against the Turks, the second against blood-sucking lice and the third against fleas. The lice infested their clothes, and drove men wild with itching and scratching. Here's a list of the troops' main ways of dealing with these tiny foes:

1. Nip 'em and squeeze 'em.
2. Burn 'em out of the seams of your clothes with candles or hot embers of the fire (try not to scorch the cloth).
3. Keatings flea powder. Problem: they seem to like it.
4. Army-issue camphor balls. Problem: they make nests in them.
5. Most ingenious weapon (promote this man to sergeant): Lay clothes over an ant's nest (there are a lot in Gallipoli) for the ants to feed on the lice. It works! But be sure to shake all the ants out, their bite is far worse than a louse's.

Dirty Flies

Think about this – but not for too long. Thousands of dead bodies, sometimes in bits, and tens of thousands of men using open ditches as toilets! Then add a plague of flies – not just a couple buzzing against the window on a hot summer's day but billions of them. The flies arrived in June and fed on the corpses, the latrines, the rubbish and the food. Ivone Kirkpatrick remembered:

I used to cover the top of a box with sugar and kill flies
en masse with a sort of home-made ping-pong racquet,
but although I often went on killing till I was tired, it
never seemed to make much difference.

Dirty Diseases

With the flies came dysentery. Imagine having violent
and crippling diarrhoea – and no proper toilets, toilet
paper or any way to keep yourself clean. By July 1915
over 1,000 men a week were so ill that they had to be
evacuated to hospitals.

Other diseases prevalent at Gallipoli were jaundice,
malaria and typhoid.

Last Man Down

The last Gallipoli veteran died in May 2002, aged 103.
Australian Alec Campbell lied about his age and joined
up when he was 16. He was one of 50,000 Anzacs
among the British-led Allied army. Alec braved heavy fire
to carry water and ammunition to the front line. He
remembered: 'It was dangerous work. Every day at least
one carrier got hit. Once we were there we didn't
expect to survive.'

The memory of the Gallipoli campaign is so important
to Australians that Prime Minister John Howard cut
short a trip to China to attend Alec's funeral service in
Tasmania. The whole country came to a halt to observe
a minute's silence at 11:00.

I Want to Go Home

I want to go home, I want to go home.

I don't want to go in the trenches no more,

Where whizzbangs and shrapnel they whistle and roar.

Take me over the sea, where the **Alleyman** can't get at
  me.

Oh my, I don't want to die, I want to go home.

I want to go home, I want to go home.

I don't want to visit la Belle France no more,

For Oh the **Jack Johnsons** they make such a roar.

Take me over the sea, where the snipers they can't get
  at me.

Oh my, I don't want to die, I want to go home.

Trench song

GUESTS OF
THE KAISER

BATTLE BRIEFING

Prisoners of War

While there are many stories of Allied prisoners in World War II, the **POWs** of World War I have been largely forgotten. Yet the total number of prisoners taken was huge, about 6.6 million. On the Western Front the Germans captured some 170,000 British soldiers and 500,000 French. On the Eastern Front many more Russians became reluctant guests of the Kaiser, including 92,000 in one week during the Battle of Tannenburg in August 1914.

The belligerents promised to follow the rules of war agreed to at the conventions of Geneva (1907) and The Hague (1908) and take reasonable care of captured enemy soldiers. In reality the long and bitter struggle often led to the mistreatment or neglect of prisoners. Life in the camps was dreary and hard, with poor food and contagious diseases, such as typhus, rife. Inmates were expected to work — to cover some of the costs of their detention — in mines, farming, factories or public services. One British prisoner at a camp in Tournai listed the many jobs he was given: 'making railways, emptying coal barges, cleaning streets, removing shells from trucks, carrying German wounded from the trains to hospital.'

Soldiers never expected to be taken prisoner and the moment of capture always came as a shock. In April 1915 Canadian Baron Richardson Racey could never have guessed that his days of freedom were almost over . . . or that his diary would tell one of the great escape stories of the war. The words in italics are his.

ESCAPE RECIPE

January 1916: Vehnemoor Prison Camp

It was a hard march to the new prison camp, 10 miles (16 km) from the station through the freezing January weather. That night Baron scribbled a quick entry in his diary: *Finally arrived more dead than alive, ate a basin of fish soup and crawled to bed on the hard boards.*

Baron kept his diary well hidden from the guards. It was his lifeline. When fits of the 'blues' left him cursing his bad luck and wondering if the war would ever end, the diary was an escape route in his head. But even

Baron had to admit that some days it made dismal reading. That night, as the cold bit through his thin blankets, those last days of freedom seemed so long ago. So full of 'if onlys' ...

April 1915: Ypres

Baron was among the first contingent of Canadians to arrive in Belgium, a private in the Royal Montreal Regiment. Looking back, the night No. 3 Company moved up to the front at Ypres seemed like an omen. It was mid-April 1915, pitch black and pouring with rain. They stumbled forwards along a long a road that was nothing but shell holes, swearing in whispers as one man after another tumbled into the muddy craters.

When they finally reached their position – the reserve trenches – life didn't improve. The dugouts were so small and cramped that the first man through the low door jammed tight, trapped by his own bulky kit. The whole company was held up while he was dragged clear by his pals, half smothered. It would have seemed funny if the odd shell hadn't been zipping overhead.

The Canadians soon learned that trench life was **nocturnal**. All the next day they were under strict orders to keep their heads down. So far German gunners hadn't located the reserve lines, and to keep it like that, if they moved they crawled. As soon as darkness fell Baron and the others set to work on new dugouts. But it was a grim experience.

*The ground was like a huge graveyard and we were
continually unearthing dead Germans. One chap dug
up a bugler and somebody got the bugle as a souvenir
and very quickly buried the* **squarehead** *again, I can
assure you.*

Digging was thirsty work, but water from nearby
streams was undrinkable. Bottles had to be carried from
the battalion water cart at St Julien, about a mile away.
No fires were allowed so there was no *beloved tea* or
hot food. Stew was brought up from the cook wagon,
*but by the time it arrived it was stone cold with about an
inch of grease on top.*

Gas Attack

A few days later the Montreals were relieved and Baron
enjoyed a break in Ypres, marvelling at the battered
remains of the Cloth Hall and enjoying the company of a
pretty Belgian girl. But the fun didn't last long. A Jack
Johnson exploded nearby and she dived into a cellar for
cover. The romance over, Baron hurried back to his unit.

There was chaos everywhere. Batteries of horse-
drawn artillery galloped past, hysterical civilians ran
around in panic and, most ominous of all, he saw dozens
of French soldiers stumbling along, gasping for breath.
This was 22 April and Baron was in the middle of the first
big German gas attack on the Western Front (see pages
42–3). The Algerians holding the line had broken, leaving

a gap 4 miles (6 km) long. As the Germans poured through, the Canadians moved up to plug the breach.

It took hard-nosed courage to advance through the fleeing French. Like their allies, the Montreals had no protection against this new weapon. Baron wrote:

> All we could get out of them was 'les Allemands vient avec le gaz asphixiant' [the Germans are coming with poisonous gas] and then they would burst into a fit of the most awful choking and stagger on a few more yards.

Around St Julien the Canadians dug in like the *busiest little moles*. Baron had just finished his foxhole when he was ordered forward with two others to locate the enemy position. Inching ahead for 600 feet (180 m) they lay in a ditch and listened carefully. German voices? Yes!

Job done, the trio started back, one at a time. Baron was last, around 120 feet (37 m) behind the others, when a stern French voice demanded to know who he was.

Now, hindsight is a wonderful thing! And the if onlys ran through his thoughts for months afterwards.

If only I'd kept quiet.

If only I'd run.

If only I'd opened fire.

> Like a damned fool, thinking they were a stray party of French, I told them in broken English and French who I was, but got the shock of my young life when about a

*dozen spiked helmets jumped up at me. One grabbed
my rifle and another my bayonet ...*

In less than the time it takes to tell, he was a prisoner.

Captivity

Baron's first night in German hands was spent locked
in a barn with two dying Algerians. They had been badly
gassed, and groaned, choked and coughed their lives
slowly away. To add to their hellish rattle, two
batteries of German guns moved in behind the farm
buildings and opened fire. By dawn he was nearly deaf
from the roar.

Next morning Baron and about a dozen others were
marched back through the captured French lines. The
memory burned vividly:

*A lovely spring morning and then you stumble across a
mangled heap of human beings, or at least all that
remained of them, some perhaps showing no wounds
at all, as if they were asleep; others hunched up into all
kinds of strange shapes.*

And soon he got his first taste of enemy hospitality – *a
damned rough time*. Some German soldiers dashed out of
their billets to look at the 'Englanders', jeering and yelling
insults; others thought the chance too good to miss,
spitting on and kicking the prisoners as they passed. In
the coming months the treatment didn't get any better.

Newly captured British POWs held in a field

The next night was spent locked in the church in the village of Staden. Officers came and went, taking photographs and asking questions, but at least they didn't hand out beatings. One old general strolled across to Baron and asked him for his Royal Montreal badges for souvenirs. Feeling it would be ill-mannered to refuse, he handed them over. By now desperate for sleep, he crawled into a confession box and got his head down.

The following day the humiliation continued. The prisoners were lined up in a column of fours to march to the station, but no sooner had they left the church than waiting German troops closed in, baying like a pack of dogs. Marching on the outside of the row, Baron was kicked black and blue. But worse was to come. At the station, the men were packed tight into cattle cars for transportation to prison camp – 60 to a car. There was no room to sit or lie down and among them were more gassed and seriously ill Algerians – many vomiting or suffering from diarrhoea. The journey took two days, and the train stopped only once for a 10-minute toilet break.

A line of British POWs being sent to prison camp in cattle trucks

Camp Memories

Following his capture, Baron was locked up in four camps, each leaving sharp memories.

Camp 1

Meschede in Westphalia, Prussia, where the 'Englanders'

were given all the worst jobs, like cleaning the drains and emptying the camp rubbish. Lunch was always soup – black bean and potato soup, dried fish and potato soup or sauerkraut and potato soup, Supper was a German delicacy – salt herring, absolutely raw. Baron noted ruefully:

> Men who had money were able to buy sausage,
> margarine and honey at the canteen. I sold everything
> I had and was dressed in rags. A tunic would fetch
> anything from five to ten marks and boots up to 20.
> I sold my hat, tunic, watch, but hung on to my boots.

Parcels sent from home or by the Red Cross were essential for extra food, luxuries and new clothes (see page 96).

Feeding prisoners. The man on the right of the large pan is using his helmet as a bowl

Camp 2

In July 1915 Baron was moved to Giessen, near Frankfurt, and with great regret staged a mini-rebellion. He was among a party of prisoners sent to live on a farm and help with the work. The farmer was kind, the food good and it was great to be away from the camp.

So why spoil it?

Baron's reasoning went like this:

> We had a great discussion as to whether it was right for us to work for the Germans ... helping them with their food supply. Half a dozen of us talked it over and decided to strike.

The Germans were furious. The prisoners were denounced as '*nichts arbeiters*' – 'won't works' – and sent straight back to camp to the punishment barracks. This meant eight hours a day standing to attention or sitting still on a stool: no cigarettes, food parcels or books – and no talking. If anyone nodded off, the guard would gleefully pour a jug of cold water down his neck.

Camp 3

Just after New Year 1916 came Cellelager in Hanover. The food was better ... well, at least the soup seemed thicker. But the camp, built on flat and swampy ground, was dismal beyond description. Baron was there only a week ... yet soon he wished it had been longer.

Camp 4

Then Vehnemoor, near Oldenburg. It made him shudder at first sight. The place was ankle deep in mud and the barracks were filthy. Three hundred prisoners were crammed in each block, sleeping in bunks three tiers high. Through the wire fence, there was nothing to see but miles and miles of bleak, waterlogged moor. For the first time Baron began to think seriously of escape.

Escape or Die

Getting out of the camps seemed the easy part. Baron had witnessed quite a few breaks for freedom, some by fellow Canadians. Yet most escapees were soon recaptured and brought back to kick their heels in the punishment cells. Why did so many attempts go wrong? For the rest of that miserable winter he made it his business to find out.

Scouring the camp, Baron chatted to every prisoner who had gone over the wire and learned important lessons from each adventure:

- If you break out in a big group split up quickly. Pairs are best.
- Stay hidden during the day.
- Take your time at the frontier. Don't get too impatient. Choose the right spot and wait.

Armed with these golden rules, Baron prepared to head for the nearest border, neutral Holland. But how was he to find the way? Little by little, he begged, borrowed and stole a bespoke escape kit:

- Compass: the essential item! Bought from a Russian for 15 marks and several shirts and sets of underwear.
- File: stolen from a workshop.
- Railway timetable with small map of Germany: generously given by another prisoner.
- Oilskin and water-wings: sent from home in a parcel. Amazingly, the Germans didn't confiscate the water-wings or even ask how much swimming practice he expected in a prison camp!
- Food: saved from Red Cross parcels.

By the spring Baron was all set, when prison life took another sudden dive. That Easter, he was sent with around 50 others to Schwansburg Bei Friesoythe to work on a huge potato farm. OK, it was 20 miles (32 km) away – 20 miles nearer the Dutch border. But that was the end of the good news.

The prisoners were met with a shocking sight when they marched into the old factory that was to be their new barracks. Baron wrote:

The building was occupied by about 50 Russians who were the most pitiable objects, their clothes in rags, no boots, just wooden sabots with no socks and straw stuck in them. Pale, lifeless-looking specimens, just existing from day to day. They had been in this camp two years, living

> on a starvation diet and working like slaves all day. They
> even had to put grass in their soup to thicken it and
> dozens of them had died the previous summer.

The condition of the Russians was a warning; this camp was to be the most brutal yet.

The guards woke the prisoners at 06:00 with cries of 'Raus, raus, austand', lashing out with sticks or rifle butts. Anyone sick was beaten out of bed and dragged along. The work was back-breaking: planting or carrying sacks of potatoes until it was hard to stand upright. No food parcels reached them for a month and the meals were dire. To survive, Baron was forced to eat his precious escape stocks. But one memory burned most of all:

> Our work was superintended by a German civvy who
> was strongly inoculated [sic] with hate of all Englanders
> . . . he used to bring out his wife at lunch time to see
> 'the swine eat', as we heard him telling her. I only hope
> it is my good fortune to get him alone in the
> backwoods . . .

Breakout

By mid-July Baron had squirrelled away new escape rations and found three willing partners: Harry Ramsay, Adzich (a **Montenegrin**) and Lovell. They planned to make a break together and then split up into pairs at the River Ems, before trying for the frontier. Every night for a week they slept with their clothes on, ready to run. Finally the night of 13 July was perfect – heavy rain and pitch black. Baron had been watching the guards on patrol for weeks and knew they had a 'gateway' between rounds.

When everyone was asleep, the budding **Houdinis** crept to the back of the barracks, through a chorus of snores and grunts. To keep the noise down each man wore three pairs of heavy socks over his boots. Kneeling

Baron Richardson Racey (second left) in the oilskin coat he was wearing when he escaped

by the back wall, they squeezed though a hole — made earlier by loosening two boards — into an adjoining outhouse. Scanning again for the guard, they edged through the door and took it in turns to climb on to the roof of the outhouse. This gave them the height they needed to jump over the perimeter wire.

Adzich went first, making such a racket that the others thought the game was up. But their luck held. He cleared the wire and dashed to the rendezvous point, a nearby shepherd's hut. Baron jumped third, leaping clear of the roof, but catching the seat of his trousers on the wire. Like a manic acrobat he dangled, wriggling furiously until his trousers tore loose. Even the loud RRRRRIP of

Escaping over the fence

cloth and TWANGGGG of wire failed to bring the guards running.

Escape Highlights
Once clear of the camp it was time to move fast, travelling at night and hiding by day. When the novelty of being free wore off, the journey became a test of endurance and nerves.

Night 1
Cloaked by lowering clouds and filthy weather, Baron and his mates headed towards a small hill, seen in the distance from the camp. At about 04:00 they took cover in a hayfield. Breakfast was a feast: bully beef and biscuits.

Scariest time: Germans working in the fields around them, so close they dare not sit up.

Night 2
As dark fell, they pushed on hard across open moors. The waterlogged ground was an obstacle course of ditches and streams. At daybreak they hid in thick woodland near a village. Baron had good cause to write about this day, as it was his birthday: *We sat down to the strangest party I shall ever experience. Instead of cake we ate some fudge sent me from a friend in Toronto.*

Scariest time: The woods were next to a main road. They could hear Germans talking as they rode past in carts.

Night 3

Shortly after the village settled down for the night the escapees crept through, armed with thick clubs made out of branches. Stopping at intervals to check the compass, they travelled on to the edge of a small town. Skirting this through fields, they crossed a main road that showed on their tiny map. Perfect! Only a few miles from the River Ems and bang on target for Holland. Relieved, they took refuge in a field of wheat for the day.

Scariest time: Being spooked by horses or cows during their night march. Baron noted: *Your heart would be in your mouth until you realized what it was, and the relief would be intense.*

Night 4

The prisoners reached the River Ems but decided to rest up before trying to cross. They slept in a wood again and, since supplies were almost gone, their meal was half an Oxo cube each and a few mouldy crumbs.

Scariest time: Two hunters out shooting rabbits almost stumbled into their hiding place.

Night 5

This was an action-packed night that quickly became a comedy of errors. Adzich, faced with crossing the Ems, admitted he couldn't swim a stroke, while Lovell complained he would get 'cramps' if he tried to swim without the help of the water-wings. There was an anxious pause for planning.

Then Harry came up with a bright idea: they could build a raft! He and Lovell tore down two field gates and cut fencing wire to bind them together. Instant raft. And Baron, being the lightest of the four, had the 'fun' of taking her for a maiden voyage. It was short and wet. The raft worked, sort of – it would carry one person if they didn't mind being partly submerged. Troubles over? No, they were just beginning ... Now this bit is complicated, so read carefully.

Blunder 1
Baron and Harry stripped and swam across the Ems, using the raft to keep their clothes dry. Except the clothes fell off and got soaked anyway.

Blunder 2
Lovell swam across using the water-wings, picked up the raft and went back for Adzich. Except he lost the raft halfway back and began to panic.

Blunder 3
Baron and Harry saw a man running along their side of the bank, flapping his arms and yelling. It was Lovell – making enough noise to attract every German patrol for miles. They calmed him down, ready to go back again for Adzich. Except the water-wings burst – and Adzich was stuck!

Blazing Row

At this point, all their anger and frustration erupted and the three men had a blazing row.

Lovell's argument: We can't desert Adzich. We must stick together, find a bridge and go and get him.

Baron's argument: All the bridges will be guarded. We might as well surrender as try to cross one. You lost the raft. Adzich is your problem.

As Baron drily wrote, *after mutual compliments had passed between us, Lovell started along the bank.* It was time to split up.

That day Baron and Harry hid in a swamp near the river ... in sopping-wet clothes ... in the pouring rain ... with no food ... and with very large slugs that crawled all over them.

Night 6

The intrepid pair travelled due west, using the stars as a guide. The border was achingly close now and sentries frequent.

Scariest moment: Caught in the open by a patrol, Baron and Harry hugged the ground, taking an hour to wriggle slowly past. Then the moon came out and the 'patrol' turned into *blocks of peat piled up about the height of a man.* Oops!

The next day dawned hot and dry. They camped in a field of rye and seized the chance to take their sodden clothes off and dry them. Their bellies rumbled but they fought off the hunger pangs by smoking the day away.

Night 7

Time for the final push to Holland — on a brilliant moonlit night.

Good point: They could see clearly.

Bad point: So could any Germans.

Checking the compass, they headed due west, across a small canal and a main road, crawling or sticking tightly to the shadows cast by tall hedges. Coming to a crossroad, Baron and Harry could hear yells and see lights flashing. With seconds to spare, they flung themselves into a ditch and lay still as a patrol marched past, rifles slung.

After a brief wait they crawled into a field and over some low mounds. Harry stopped and gave Baron a kick. The mounds were freshly dug graves! As if to prove the point, shots rang out in the dark and someone gave a bloodcurdling yell. Sentries dashed to and fro. Was it some other poor devil heading for the border? Taking a chance, they sprinted for cover in the garden of a nearby house. Problems enough, you'd think, but then Harry whispered, 'For God's sake, look over the hedge.' Glinting in the moonlight were two anchored airships. They had blundered into a makeshift German aerodrome.

Baron and Harry spent the rest of the night huddled in a shrubbery until dawn, when another shock awaited them. The house had been converted into the airfield HQ. All the glass in the upper windows had been taken out and a wooden platform had been built on the roof. This had a gun mounted on it. If they were caught now they were likely to be shot as spies, never mind rearrested as escapees.

In a desperate situation they fell back on the boldest of plans. Waiting till local workers were on the move, they stood up and walked out of the garden. Trying to look part of the scenery, the pals coolly lit cigarettes and strolled behind two men carrying dinner pails. Incredibly it worked. They were given a few suspicious glances but no one stopped them. Some friendly civilians even grunted 'Good morning' and seemed content with the 'Ja, ja' Baron growled in return.

The rest of the day was spent heading west, always looking for quiet lanes. At a railway crossing a soldier walking the tracks stared at them, but let them go unchallenged. Why, Baron couldn't guess. Even to his eyes they seemed shady: *Two awful-looking scarecrows – nine days' beard, not washed, sleeping anywhere in mud, clothes torn by barbed wire.*

At last they sat down by a wood and Baron picked up a scrap of newspaper – the language was Dutch. They looked in astonishment. Had they crossed the border without even realizing, or had the paper blown some distance? There was only one way to check. When an old farmer ambled past with a few cows, they stepped out and asked in German which country they were in, Germany or Holland. 'Nederland,' came the reply.

The farmer watched in amazement as the two scarecrows danced in the road. They'd made it!

FIGHTING FACTS

What Happened to Baron?

Baron survived the war fit and well. It was Canadian army policy not to send prisoners back to the front, so he returned to civilian life as a bank clerk. With the war still raging, he was eager to join up again and made repeated applications to the new Naval Air Arm. By the time he had been taken on for pilot training, however, the fighting in Europe was over.

In World War II Baron was back in uniform, as a major in the Veterans Guard of Canada, and in a way fate turned full circle. He found himself the commanding officer of an internment camp for Austrian Jews, refugees held in camps in case they were enemy agents. Needless to say, his own experiences gave him plenty of sympathy with their plight.

What Happened to Lovell and Adzich?

Did you think that Baron was a bit hard on Lovell and Adzich when they split up? Well, you can stop worrying.

Baron Richardson Racey, c 1942

By a stroke of luck, Lovell found a boat about a quarter of a mile away and got Adzich across the river. They made it to Holland too.

Young Lions

When Britain went to war in 1914 the peoples of the Dominions, Canada, Australia, New Zealand and India, joined the struggle. The Canadian record was remarkable. From a population of only 8 million, 619,636 men and women joined up. Of these 66,655 were killed, while another 172,950 became casualties.

The fighting spirit of Canadian troops was second to none. During the deadly German breakthrough on 22 April at Ypres, they counter-attacked and held the crumbling line until reinforcements arrived. Two days later the Germans struck again and this time their target was the Canadians. As the gas cloud billowed over, the defenders were left gasping for air through mud-soaked handkerchiefs, but they were not driven back. The cost, however, was high: 6,035 Canadian men died – one in three of those in the battle.

Red Cross Aid

The International Committee of the Red Cross (ICRC), based in neutral Switzerland, tried to make sure warring nations followed the rules of the Geneva Convention. Red Cross officials visited hundreds of POW camps and checked the standards of food,

A recruiting poster appealing for help from the Empire

hygiene and prisoners' quarters. The ICRC had no powers to force countries to improve conditions, but it could try to embarrass them into better treatment by making its reports public.

From the prisoners' point of view the Red Cross organized one marvellous service — parcels of food, clothing and other luxuries — and they'd sent out almost 2 million by the end of the war. A food parcel was designed to weigh 13 lb (6 kg) and soldiers could expect to be sent two every fortnight. Each one was like a mini Christmas present and included cocoa, tea, cigarettes, biscuits, cheese and tinned milk.

For many prison inmates, including Baron, they made the difference between health and malnutrition. Baron recalled his many hunger pangs:

> The first card I sent home simply said, 'I am a prisoner' and, well, the second one was filled up with request for grub. You could bet your boots if you saw a party of Englishmen talking together the subject was GRUB with a capital G, either describing with full details the last large juicy steak they had, or the last Christmas dinner . . . I used to dream of maple sugar and buckwheat pancakes.

Parcel Problems
Parcels were often searched, because early in the war there had been cases of families and friends hiding

escape kits: files or saws in packets of sugar or compasses in tins of cigarettes. This had made camp commandants uneasy, especially if they were close to the Dutch border. Later, it was common for guards to steal parcels. By 1918 there were severe shortages in Germany and many civilians were close to starvation. Women and children were even seen begging through the barbed wire for food from prisoners. Parcels were also used to punish prisoners: bad behaviour, no parcels.

Did the Germans Really Hate British Prisoners?

Baron complains bitterly of German harshness towards British prisoners, but was their treatment really worse than average? He may have a point! Early in the war German troops disliked the British because they were professional soldiers or – even worse – volunteers, not conscripts like themselves. In the eyes of some, this made them little better than mercenaries (hired killers). Later in the war, when the Royal Navy blockade led to widespread food shortages in Germany, British soldiers were blamed. One wounded prisoner remembered that, as he lay on the operating table, he was asked what kind of soldier he was. When he replied that he was a regular, the surgeon said, 'Good. If you had been a volunteer I would not have operated on you.' So you can well imagine what the Germans thought of Canadian volunteers who had sailed 3,000 miles to get into a European war!

However, if the Germans disliked the British it was the Russians they really detested. So many Russian prisoners fell into German hands that they couldn't cope and tens of thousands died of malnutrition or from diseases such as dysentery. The condition of the Russians seen by Baron was all too typical.

Bombed Last Night

Bombed last night, and bombed the night before.
Going to get bombed tonight if we never get bombed
any more.
When we're bombed, we're scared as can be.
Can't stop the bombing from old Higher Germany.

They're warning us, they're warning us.
One shell hole for just the four of us.
Thank your lucky stars there are no more of us.
So one of us can fill it alone.

Gassed last night, and gassed the night before.
Going to get gassed tonight if we never get gassed any
more.
When we're gassed we're sick as can be.
For phosgene and mustard gas is too much for me.

They're killing us, they're killing us.
One respirator between the four of us.
Thank your lucky stars that we can all run fast.
So one of us can take it all alone.

Trench song

THE PRISONERS' MARTYR – EDITH CAVELL

BATTLE BRIEFING

A Women's War

World War I transformed the role of women in Britain. Although they were not called up and did not fight, they did play a vital support role in the war effort. About 1.5 million women went into industry to replace the men who had joined up and to supply the vast range of equipment the armed services needed, everything from uniforms and rifles to artillery and ammunition. They took on a host of jobs – as engineers, carpenters, plumbers, crane drivers, munitions workers and bus or tram conductors – often tackling skilled work done only by men before.

Other women, however, wanted to get closer to the action and help the men who were suffering. Between 1914 and 1918 around 23,000 served as nurses and 15,000 as orderlies of the Voluntary Aid Detachment. Most worked in military hospitals in England but several thousand served in field hospitals close to the front lines and saw the full cost of the war. They dealt with men whose limbs had been shattered by shellfire or whose lungs had been seared by poisonous gas.

Not surprisingly, some nurses broke down under the stress of the horrors they witnessed and were forced to leave. But most found a way to cope and stayed, buoyed up by a sense of duty. In 1915 one story became an inspiration for a whole generation of young women.

EDITH CAVELL

A Sense of Duty

In early August 1914 Edith Cavell was in Norwich on a short holiday from her nurses' training college in Belgium. She had come to visit her elderly mother and was enjoying the warm summer weather. Edith was in the garden, digging weeds, when she heard the news that excited all Europe: war had been declared and German troops were massed on the Belgian border. Her response was instant: 'At a time like this I am needed more than ever.' Protests from friends and family fell on deaf ears.

Edith Cavell in uniform

Edith knew where her duty lay. She must return to Brussels as soon as possible ... whatever the risks.

Duty was the thread that ran through the life of Edith Louisa Cavell. Born in 1865, she was the daughter of the vicar of Swardeston, a small village in Norfolk. Although the Cavells lived in an imposing vicarage, keeping up appearances was not easy and money was always short. One disgruntled maid scribbled on an attic bedroom wall: 'The pay is small, the food is bad, I wonder why I don't go mad.' Even so, the family shared what they had. When Sunday lunch was served a portion of the joint was always sent to poor and hungry villagers.

The situation of the Cavell family meant that Edith had to earn her own living. At 16 she began training as a pupil teacher and showed a gift for French. Three years later she became a governess – a respectable job for a middle-class girl. After working with English families for a few years, Edith's sense of adventure led her abroad. In 1890 she took a job with the François family in Brussels and enjoyed life in Belgium. In 1895, however, her father became seriously ill and she returned home to nurse him – sowing the seed for the next change in her life.

A Caring Career

Edith had been looking for a greater challenge, a career that would allow her to help more people, and at the age of 30 she decided to go into nursing. It was not an easy choice. In 1896 she began training at the London Hospital under the stern eye of Eva Lückes. Hours were long, 07:00 to 21:00, with only half an hour for lunch. And Edith did not impress her tutor. Miss Lückes observed witheringly: 'Edith Louisa Cavell had plenty of capacity for her work, when she chose to exert herself . . . she was not at all punctual.'

The following year, however, Edith redeemed herself. She was part of an emergency team of six nurses sent to help with an outbreak of typhoid fever at Maidstone. Thanks to their care, out of 1,700 patients who caught the disease, only 132 died.

In 1907 Edith's Belgian connections led to an offer she couldn't refuse. Dr Antoine Lepage was trying to set up a new school to train nurses at the Berkendael Institute near Brussels and he needed an able matron who could speak French. Edith was recommended to him by one of the François children, now grown up and married, and he eagerly interviewed her. An English nurse who could bring the ideas of Florence Nightingale to Belgium would be perfect.

The job was a challenge. As in England a generation before, Belgian mothers from 'good families' were horrified at the idea of their daughters becoming nurses. It took time, hard work and patience to break through this snobbery. One reason for Edith's success was her dedication to her work. Students remembered her as a brisk and businesslike woman in her forties, with high expectations. She kept a watch on the table in front of her at breakfast, and any girl more than two minutes late would be ordered to work an extra two hours. By 1912 the Berkendael Institute had become a modern teaching hospital, providing nurses for three other hospitals, 24 schools and 13 kindergartens.

War Zone

That fateful August in 1914 Edith quickly returned to Brussels and shared the nightmare that hit the Belgian people over the next few weeks. The German army invaded on 4 August; by the 16th the mighty Liège forts had been stormed; Brussels was captured on the 20th; and the British army sent reeling back from Mons on the 23rd. One bewildered German soldier wrote:

> When one sees the wasting, burning villages and towns, plundered cellars and attics, dead or half-starved animals, cattle bellowing in the sugar beet fields and then corpses, corpses, corpses . . . then everything becomes a lunacy.

With heavy fighting nearby, the institute became a Red Cross hospital, meaning that wounded from both sides could be treated without the staff facing repercussions.

Soon after Brussels fell, the Germans ordered 60 British nurses to return home, but Edith and one English assistant, Sister White, were allowed to stay behind and continue their work with their Belgian staff. The German authorities believed that since Edith was working under the banner of the Red Cross, she would remain strictly **neutral**. But within weeks she was forced to choose between her conscience and her neutrality. During September a young Belgian engineer called Herman Capiau visited Edith. He told her a harrowing tale: dozens of British soldiers trapped behind enemy lines had been sheltered by Belgian civilians, but at great risk. The Germans, determined to cow the Belgians into submission, were hunting down these stragglers and sometimes shooting them, together with any civilian who had dared to hide them. Warily, Edith agreed to help liberate these soldiers.

A piecemeal **resistance movement** soon sprang up to fight back against this harsh rule. The Prince and Princess de Croy, together with a trusted group of brave Belgians, built an escape network to help British soldiers get across the border to Holland. Since the only hope of liberating Belgium lay in an Allied victory, the more men they sent back to the war the better. But, just as importantly, they assisted many Belgian and French men of fighting age to flee the German-occupied zones and join up. The network password was Yorc – Croy backwards.

Going Underground

On 1 November Herman Capiau put Edith's offer to the test. Now a key worker in the de Croy organization, he urgently needed a bolt hole for two British soldiers. Like many others, Lieutenant-Colonel Dudley Bolger and Company Sergeant-Major Frank Meachin, both from the Cheshire Regiment, had been cut off as the British army retreated from Mons. They had been lucky enough to be taken in by an elderly woman, Mrs Libiez, who hid them in an outbuilding in her garden for several weeks – until an informer tipped off the Germans. Dudley and Frank escaped just in time. They managed to slip out of the back door and mingle with crowds of local civilians just as a company of **Landsturm** cycle troops swooped on their hideout.

A desperate game of hide-and-seek began as the network passed the soldiers from **safe house** to safe house. And into the hands of Herman Capiau. On a grey and dismal autumn night, Herman led them through the streets of Brussels to the Berkendael Institute. German patrols seemed to be everywhere, but their disguises worked. Dudley wore the black hat and floppy tie of an ordinary Belgian factory worker, while Frank flamboyantly squashed rolls of cloth between his shoulders blades, so he looked like a hunchback. This way, if anyone asked why a tall, well-built man was not in the army he had a ready excuse.

It was a little before 20:00 when the three arrived on Edith's doorstep, but it never crossed her mind to turn them away.

'These men are fugitive soldiers,' she told Sister White. 'Give them beds in the empty surgical house.'

Exhausted and dirty, but highly relieved, Dudley and Frank were soon sound asleep in crisp white sheets.

Edith hid the escapees for two weeks – until she had warning that the Germans were going to search the institute. Sister White took them to an empty house on the nearby Avenue Louise, where they stayed before being moved on. Finally, a guide escorted them out of the city, to the canal path leading to Ghent. Frank was lucky. He made friends with a Belgian who smuggled newspapers across the border from Holland. With the smuggler's help, he reached the frontier and dashed to safety. Dudley was caught when a German patrol searched a café where he had stopped to have a drink. He was sent to a prisoner of war camp at Ruhleben, Germany, and spent the rest of the war behind barbed wire.

Belgium, Holland, France and Germany

For Edith this deadly adventure was just the beginning. Frank and Dudley were the first of more than 200 fugitives she sheltered at the institute in the coming months.

Arrest

In May 1915 Edith received heartbreaking news. The liner *Lusitania* had been sunk by a German submarine and her friend Madame Lepage had drowned. She was the wife of the doctor who founded the institute and was returning from a fund-raising mission to the USA. This toughened Edith's resolve to fight on, but already the network was starting to unravel. The Germans were suspicious and the evidence was mounting.

In an act of incredible stupidity, a group of British soldiers sheltering at the institute had sneaked out to a nearby café and got drunk. Everyone in the neighbourhood now knew what was going on and some tongues wagged. Compounding this, one soldier who made it back to England sent Edith a postcard ... with his thanks!

Worst of all, one escapee helped by the network turned out to be a **collaborator** and the institute was searched several times. Coolly, Edith had sewn up her diary in a cushion to avoid detection.

On 31 July 1915 the end came suddenly. The house of Philippe Baucq, a key figure in the network, was raided. Philippe was detained and incriminating letters, with

Edith's name in them, were seized before he could destroy them. Shortly afterwards, Prince de Croy visited Edith with alarming news: he was going into hiding, before fleeing to Holland, and she should do the same. Her reply was forthright: 'I expect to be arrested. Escape for me is futile and unthinkable.' Perhaps it was stubbornness, perhaps her sense of duty, perhaps a dogged urge to defy the Germans, but Edith did not run.

On 5 August the Germans came for her, led by Otto Mayer of the secret police. After three days of intense questioning, the German interrogators tried a new approach. 'We know everything,' they told her. 'Thirty-five members of the network have been arrested and they have confessed. We will go easy with them if you cooperate.'

Naively, Edith believed what she was told and made a full confession, pouring out names, dates and places. Later she wrote in a letter: 'Had I not helped they would have been shot.'

Edith was locked up in the prison of St Giles until her trial before a German military court in October. The United States Ambassador in Belgium, Brand Whitlock, scornfully described what such trials were like:

The secret police would bring before the bench of German officers all the evidence as they called it ... The court would admit hearsay, presumptions, inferences and innuendoes so long as they were on the part of the prosecution. The accused was sometimes allowed to present a defence but it was only such as he might contrive in sparring with the judges.

Edith came to trial on Thursday 7 October, alongside the others who had been rounded up. The court sat for just 48 hours but the judges were impressed by Edith's forthright honesty. When asked if she had helped 20 soldiers to escape she replied, 'Yes. More than 20, 200.'

'English?'

'No, not all English. French and Belgians too.'

But her courage was not the issue. In the eyes of the army judges Edith had committed treason. On Monday 11 October they pronounced her sentence: death by firing squad, to be carried out the next day at the Tir Nationale, the National Rifle Range. But she was not to die alone. Philippe Baucq would be shot alongside her. That night she told Stirling Gahn, the English priest allowed to visit her, 'I know that patriotism is not enough. I must have no hatred and no bitterness towards anyone.'

Edith and Philippe were woken at dawn and driven to the execution ground in an army motor car. Edith was wearing her white nursing uniform. The firing squads presented arms and the sentence was read out in German and French. Philippe yelled in a clear voice, 'Comrades, in the presence of death we are all comrades.' He was not allowed to say any more. A

German chaplain, Pasteur Le Seur, comforted Edith. He recalled:

> I took Miss Cavell's hand and said in English, 'The Grace of our Lord Jesus Christ and the love of God and the Communion of the Holy Spirit be with you for ever. Amen.' She pressed my hand in return and answered, 'Ask Mr Gahn to tell my loved ones that my soul, as I believe, is safe, and that I am glad to die for my country.' Then I led her a few steps to a pole, to which she was loosely bound. A bandage was put over her eyes which, as the soldier who put it on told me, were full of tears.

Seconds later the shots rang out and Edith's body slumped forward. One bullet had gone through her forehead. Death was quick.

FIGHTING FACTS

Outrage

Although the German execution of Edith Cavell was justified according to the rules of war, it was a costly mistake. Both the American and Spanish ambassadors had pleaded for her life, stressing the way she had helped the wounded of both sides, but they were ignored. When the news of Edith's execution broke,

MURDERED

OCTOBER 12TH, 1915

By THE Huns

MISS EDITH CAVELL

ENLIST IN THE 99th

AND HELP STOP SUCH ATROCITIES

PUBLISHED BY THE ESSEX COUNTY RECRUITING COMMITTEE

The execcution of Edith outraged Britain and led to angry posters like this

public opinion across the world was outraged. The USA became more sympathetic to the Allied cause, while in Britain recruitment doubled for eight weeks after her death was announced.

Today the memory of Edith Cavell is still honoured. In 1919 her body was brought home and buried in Norwich Cathedral. Each year a memorial service is held to recall her bravery and sacrifice. In Canada Mount Edith Cavell, a mountain in the Jasper National Park, Alberta, was named in tribute to her.

Gallant Little Belgium

On 2 August 1914 Germany demanded the right to march a huge army through Belgian territory to deliver a knockout blow against France. When this was refused the Germans invaded anyway, on the night of 3–4 August. It was this attack on a small, neutral country that brought Britain into the war. Lord Baden-Powell, the founder of the Scout movement, summed up the public mood when he compared Belgium to a plucky little tailor set upon by 'a big beery loafer'.

During the war Belgium suffered terribly. The German attack was fast and brutal. The ancient university library at Louvain went up in flames, while 600 civilians were shot at Dinant after snipers fired on passing German troops. When the capital, Brussels, fell on 20 August the government moved to Antwerp and finally to Le Havre in France. Before the end of October 1914, most of the

Recruiting poster

115

country was occupied and a million civilians became refugees, with over 100,000 fleeing to Britain. By 1917 many of those who had stayed behind were desperate. In Brussels alone, one third of the 750,000 people living in the city were penniless and kept alive only by soup kitchens.

Eyewitness: A Nurse's View

Edith was not alone during the dreadful weeks of 1914 when most of Belgium was conquered. Dozens of British nurses were close to the fighting. One published her diary anonymously in 1918, with the title *Sketches from a Belgian Field Hospital*. She served through the siege of Antwerp and left this moving description of evacuating wounded from the shattered city in a London bus commandeered by the army:

> Have you ever ridden in a London motor bus? If not, I can give you little idea what our poor wounded suffered. To begin with, even traversing the smooth London streets these vehicles jolt you to bits, whilst the smell of burnt gasoline is stifling, so just imagine these unwieldy things bumping along over cobblestones and loose sandy ruts of rough tracks among the sand-dunes. When you have the picture before you just think of the passengers – not healthy people on a penny bus ride, but wounded soldiers and sailors. Upon the brow of many, death had set his seal. All those inside

passengers were either wounded in the abdomen, shot through the lungs or pierced through the skull, often with their brains running out through the wound, whilst we had more than one case of men with broken backs. Many of these we had just operated upon.

My Boy Jack

'Have you news of my boy Jack?'
Not this tide.
'When do you think he'll come back?'
Not with this wind blowing and this tide.

'Had anyone else had word of him?'
Not this tide
For what is sunk will hardly swim,
Not with this wind blowing, and this tide.

'Oh, dear, what comfort can I find?'
None this tide,
Nor any tide,
Except he did not shame his kind —
Not even with that wind blowing, and that tide.

Then hold up your head up all the more,
This tide,
And every tide;
Because he was the son you bore,
And gave to that wind blowing and that tide!

Rudyard Kipling

AFTERMATH

The Unknown Warrior

When World War I came to an end, Britain was a nation in mourning. With 743,00 dead and over 1,500,000 injured, almost every family had suffered terribly. Yet some faced an extra agony – the relatives and friends of men who simply vanished. Every battle left thousands of bodies so badly disfigured they couldn't be identified, while other soldiers were simply blown apart by artillery fire. One famous father who never recovered from the loss of his only son, 'My Boy Jack', was the author Rudyard Kipling. Jack's body was never found and Rudyard spent years interviewing survivors to try and trace him.

In 1919 the suggestion was made to bring home the body of an unidentified soldier for reburial in Britain. This would become a national memorial and a symbol for all the others who had no grave. The original idea came from the vicar of Margate, the Reverend David Railton, a former army chaplain who had served in France. Years later he recalled the poignant moment in 1916 that inspired him:

> I went to a billet in front of Erkingham, near Armentières. At the back was a small garden and in the garden, only six paces from the house, there was a grave. At the head of the grave there stood a rough cross of white wood. On the cross was written in deep black-pencilled letters, 'An Unknown Soldier' and in brackets beneath 'of the Black Watch'. It was dusk and no one was near, except some officers in the billet playing cards. I remember how still it was. Even the guns seemed to be resting. How that grave made me think ...

It took a year for the War Office to agree but in 1920 the plan went ahead. Brigadier General Wyatt, the officer who had commanded British troops in France and Flanders, chose the body. Four unidentified corpses were dug up and brought to the chapel at his HQ at St Pol. They came from four battle areas – the Aisne, the Somme, Arras and Ypres. Each body was draped in a Union Jack and laid on a stretcher. Wyatt pointed at one and helped to lift it into a plain, inner coffin. The other three were reburied in a nearby military cemetery.

The next day, 9 November, the Unknown Warrior began his journey home. The simple coffin was placed in a magnificent oak sarcophagus, cut from a tree in the grounds of Hampton Court Palace. On top was fixed a crusader-style sword presented by King George V.

In memory of their joint losses, a guard of French cavalry escorted the Unknown Warrior to Boulogne. There he was placed on a British destroyer, the *Verdun*, for the journey across the Channel. The warship had been named in tribute to the hard-fought battle that cost the lives of 160,000 Frenchmen.

As the *Verdun* arrived in Dover, a nineteen-gun salute rang out. Crowds gathered at every station on the line to London to watch the train carrying the body steam past. The *Daily Mail* reported, 'The train thundered

Bringing the Unknown Warrior to England from Boulogne, 11 November 1920

The King placing a wreath on the coffin of the Unknown Warrior at the Cenotaph

through a dark, wet, moonless night. At the platforms by which it rushed could be seen groups of women watching and silent, many dressed in deep mourning.'

On the morning of 11 November 1920 the coffin was placed on a gun carriage and drawn by six black horses to Whitehall. There, on the last stroke of 11:00 the King unveiled the new **Cenotaph,** designed by the architect Edward Lutyens. As the chimes died away the crowds fell silent for two minutes and the last post sounded.

The war correspondent Philip Gibbs captured the mood of many ex-soldiers when he wrote:

It did not seem an unknown warrior whose body came down Whitehall. He was known to us all. It was one of 'our boys' – not warriors – as we called them. To some women weeping a little in the crowd after an all-night vigil, he was their own boy who went missing and was never found till now. To many men wearing ribbons and badges in civilian clothes he was one of their comrades.

The solemn procession continued to Westminster Abbey, where the nave was lined with the greatest guard of honour ever seen in Britain – 100 holders of the Victoria Cross. In contrast to this military splendour, the congregation was mainly widows and

The ceremony to seal the grave of the Unknown Warrior in Westminster Abbey

Veterans at the Cenotaph today

grieving mothers. As the coffin was placed in the grave the King scattered it with soil from the battlefields of France. By the time the grave was finally closed, on 18 November, over 1 million people had visited the abbey to pay their last respects.

The Casualties

Countries	Total Mobilized	Dead	Wounded	Prisoners & Missing	Total Casualties	Casualties % of Mobilized
Allied Powers						
Russia	12,000,000	1,700,000	4,950,000	2,500,000	9,150,000	76.3
France	8,410,000	1,357,800	4,266,000	537,000	6,160,800	73.6
British Empire	8,904,467	908,371	2,090,212	191,652	3,190,235	35.8
Italy	5,615,000	650,000	947,000	600,000	2,197,000	39.1
United States	4,355,000	126,000	234,300	4,500	364,800	8.4
Romania	750,000	335,706	120,000	80,000	535,706	71.4
Serbia	707,343	45,000	133,148	152,958	331,106	46.8
Belgium	267,000	13,716	44,686	34,659	93,061	34.9
Central Powers						
Germany	11,000,000	1,773,700	4,216,058	1,152,800	7,142,558	64.9
Austria-Hungary	7,800,000	1,200,000	3,620,000	2,200,000	7,020,000	90.0
Turkey	2,850,000	325,000	400,000	250,000	975,000	34.2
Bulgaria	1,200,000	87,500	152,390	27,029	266,919	22.2

FIGHTING FACTS

War Poets

Between the chapters there is a trench song or a poem – a tiny sample of the thousands written during and after the war. With millions of men and women in combat, there was a stunning outburst of creativity as people struggled to make sense of their experiences. If you want to find out more, search for 'Trench Songs' or 'War Poets' on the Internet. Look out for authors such as Siegfried Sassoon, who won the Military Cross and suffered from shell shock; Wilfred Owen, who was killed on 4 November 1918, just one week before the war ended; or Robert Graves, who also wrote one of the best wartime biographies, *Goodbye to All That*. Most of the soldiers' songs are anonymous, but you'll notice how funny, ironic and often very rude they are. They reflect the bravery and steadfastness of the armed forces of the British Empire throughout the four years of bitter fighting.

All Over Again

Twenty-one years after World War I ended, World War II broke out between Britain and Hitler's Germany. Old soldiers joked that the bell had sounded for round two. This time the fighting spread over many countries in Europe, Africa and the Far East. It took six long years before peace came again.

Commemoration on the Web

Do you have a relative who died in World War I? You can keep alive their memory by looking them up on the *Debt of Honour Register* compiled by the Commonwealth War Graves Commission at www.cwgc.org/.

TRENCH TALK

barrage artillery bombardment.

Blighty army slang for Britain. A 'blighty one' was a wound bad enough to get a soldier sent home.

Boche rude nickname for the Germans, picked up from French soldiers

bully beef tinned corned beef, the main source of protein in a soldier's rations.

Fritz British nickname for the Germans.

exaspirator nickname for a gas mask.

Hun unsavoury nickname for a German, after the barbaric Huns of history.

Jack Johnson nickname for the fearsome German 150-mm heavy howitzer shells, infamous for their noise and black smoke. Johnson was the first black American heavyweight boxing champion, from 1909 to 1915.

Maconochie tinned meat and vegetable stew, named after the packing company. A top medal for bravery was the Military Medal or MM. Troops joked this was the Maconochie Medal, a reward for eating the stew.

mess tin a metal dish that was used as a plate, cup and cooking pan.

Montenegrin a person who lives in Montenegro, a small country in the Balkans that fought on the Allied side.

morning hate (or evening hate): an exchange of artillery fire by both sides, often at dawn or dusk.

no man's land neutral ground between the two front lines.

potato masher a German stick grenade.

puttee a cloth strip wound round the leg from ankle to

knee as a legging.

squarehead Canadian nickname for German soldiers.

star shell a shell that explodes high in the air, lighting up the landscape at night to detect sneak attacks.

Tommy German nickname for a British soldier.

whizzbang a light shell, it went whizz . . . and then bang.

PART 2

STORIES FROM THE AIR

To Andrew and Joseph,
who usually have their dad in the air

INTRODUCTION

A WORLD WAR

In August 1914 Europe went to war, with the Allies – Britain, France and Russia taking on the Central Powers – Germany and Austria-Hungary. Hopes of a short, sharp conflict were soon dashed as the opposing armies dug in on the Western Front – over 400 miles (600 km) of trenches stretching from the Swiss border to the English Channel. New and terrible weapons, especially artillery and machine guns, brought a bloody stalemate and the deaths of millions.

In four years of grim struggle, the war affected most of the world. Troops from all over the Empire – India, Canada, New Zealand and Australia – flocked to Britain's aid, while Algerians and Africans fought alongside the French. On the Eastern Front, after three years of hard fighting, the Russian government collapsed and there was a **communist revolution**.

In the war at sea, the Royal Navy rounded up or sank German raiders, and after the Battle of Jutland penned the enemy High Seas fleet into the Baltic. But enemy submarines, the sinister U-boats, were far harder to beat. Britain came close to starvation in 1917 because the U-boats sank so many ships carrying vital supplies of food.

The bloodshed was carried across the Alps when Italy declared war on the Allied side in 1915, while in the Middle East, Turkey joined the Germans. Soon British troops were battling the Turks in Mesopotamia (Iraq), Palestine, Arabia and the fatal, rocky shores of Gallipoli. In 1917 the USA joined the war, but it wasn't until the summer of 1918 that American soldiers arrived in large numbers in Europe. They came just in time to help the Allies break the last great German attack and turn defeat into victory.

War in the Air

Against this epic background a new type of combat was born – war in the air. But in August 1914 few could have guessed how momentous this would be. In Britain, the Royal Flying Corps (RFC) was a tiny branch of the army, with only 197 pilots and a few dozen planes. For most generals, aircraft were nothing more than a gimmick – at best, a cavalry patrol in the skies. Within months, however, aeroplanes had changed the face of warfare for ever.

Reconnaissance planes brought back vital information

about the movement of enemy troops and forced both sides to move their men and supplies by night. By 1915 aircraft equipped with radios could direct artillery fire, while intelligence officers pored over the details of the latest aerial photographs. Control of the skies became essential to victory and both sides developed ever more sophisticated fighting machines.

On 1 April 1918 the RFC became the Royal Air Force (RAF), Britain's third armed service and independent of the army. By this time the ramshackle squadrons of 1914 had been transformed. The RAF had more than 4,000 combat aircraft on the Western Front and 114,000 personnel. But the cost was high. In four years of fighting, Britain had trained a total of 22,000 pilots and more than half of these brave men were killed or injured. Civilians, too, were no longer secure behind the front lines. In a grim development, enemy airships and bombers had launched terror attacks into the heart of British cities.

This book highlights six stunning stories from the war in which aircraft came of age, and gives you the fighting facts behind them.

• *Cavalry in the Clouds*

In August 1914 the tiny RFC flies to France and finds itself in the path of a German knockout blow. But will anyone believe the pilots' reports of massive enemy troop movements?

• *A Strange Affair with a Machine Gun*
On 10 May 1915 Louis Strange is hanging from his plane by his fingertips – 8,000 feet (2,500 m) in the air. How did his obsession with machine guns lead to this predicament?

• *Airship Killer*
In 1915 German airships roam the skies over England. Are they really invulnerable to attack by aeroplanes or can they be stopped? One man is going to try ...

• *Gotha Summer*
In the summer of 1917 giant German bombers raid London and kill innocent civilians. Will the shock of these terror raids force the British to surrender?

• *Ace of Aces*
New pilot Edward 'Mick' Mannock seems boastful yet nervous. If he can overcome his flight nerves he has all the makings of a top-scoring ace. Will he be able to do it?

• *Sixty to One*
With the end of the war in sight, Canadian ace William Barker battles alone against a formation of 60 German planes. Can he possibly make it back home?

If your reading stalls or goes into a spin, help is at hand. Words shown in **bold** type are explained in RFC Lingo or the Glossary at the end of this book.

The performance of British aircraft is given in imperial measurements in these stories – the feet and miles per hour that the men of the RFC understood. You can convert them to metric measurements of speed and height using these tables.

Height

Feet	Metres
1,000	305
2,000	609
3,000	914
4,000	1,219
5,000	1,523
6,000	1,828
7,000	2,133
8,000	2,437
9,000	2,742
10,000	3,047
11,000	3,351
12,000	3,656
13,000	3,961
14,000	4,265
15,000	4,570
16,000	4,875
17,000	5,179
18,000	5,484
19,000	5,789
20,000	6,093
21,000	6,398

Speed

Miles per hour (mph)	Kilometres per hour (kph)
10	16
20	32
30	48
40	64
50	80
60	97
70	113
80	129
90	145
100	161
120	177
130	193
140	225
150	241

Song

We are the RFC
We cannot fight
We cannot shoot
What bloody use are we?
But when we reach Berlin
The Kaiser he will say
Mein Gott! Mein Gott!
What a jolly fine lot
Are the boys of the RFC.

Anon.

CAVALRY IN THE CLOUDS

BATTLE BRIEFING

Flying Fears

In 1903 Wilbur and Orville Wright made the first heavier-than-air flight at Kitty Hawk, North Carolina. For a feeble 12 seconds their plane skimmed across the sandy dunes. It hardly seemed a world-shaking event.

Yet within a few years the technology of flight had the British government worried. In 1908 a giant German airship flew 240 miles in 12 hours and the following year Frenchman Louis Blériot hopped from Calais to Dover in 37 minutes. Could it be that the Royal Navy and the Channel were no longer enough to make Britain safe from attack?

In 1912 the RFC was formed and the British finally began to take air power seriously. The main task of the RFC was to support the army, but there were few pilots and only a handful of planes. The service had to be built almost from scratch. It was ready, but only just, when Britain declared war on Germany on 4 August 1914.

The RFC wings proudly worn by British pilots

No one, least of all the generals, believed planes made from wood and fabric could be effective weapons. Their job was not to attack enemy troops – it was reconnaissance. Pilots were expected to be little more than aerial taxi drivers – the important men in the sky were the observers. What the army wanted from the RFC was the chance to spy out enemy troop movements, gun positions and defences – a job previously done by cavalry patrols. Soon, however, airmen would stop waving when they passed an enemy plane and start shooting.

OFF TO FRANCE

On 9 August 1914 the British Expeditionary Force (BEF)

– 80,000 men, 30,000 horses and 315 field guns – began their embarkation for France. With transports leaving every 10 minutes from Portsmouth and Southampton, the Channel seemed choked with ships. This has been called 'the best army ever to leave Britain' – highly trained and well equipped. When they landed, the smiling soldiers were given a heroes' welcome. But such good times would be short-lived. Already, complex war plans were unfolding.

The French had launched their main attack against Germany in Alsace-Lorraine. They believed their fighting spirit would soon break the enemy and sweep them on to Berlin. To support France, the British agreed to take up a covering position just inside the border of Belgium. It was a fateful move. The BEF marched smack into the path of a mighty German right hook – an army of 750,000 smashing through Belgium to encircle the French and bring the war to a rapid end.

In the face of this hammer blow, what possible use would a few dozen underpowered aeroplanes be? The army was about to find out ...

Learning the Lessons of War

Following hard on the heels of the BEF, the infant RFC prepared to go into battle. And like the British Army, it faced an impressive enemy. The Germans had 246 planes and seven airships, by far the largest air force of the European powers. Against this the RFC was tiny, with

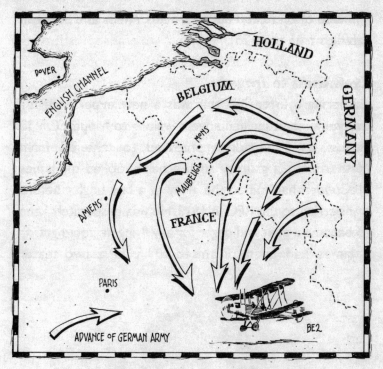

The dramatic German advance through Belgium, 1914

only four fully operational squadrons – 48 planes. But if enthusiasm counted, they would make their mark!

The journey to France was organized in a madcap hurry. First, the planes were to fly from their home airfields and gather at Dover, then they would cross the Channel in an aerial flotilla – the biggest flight of aircraft ever seen in Britain. And what a mixed bunch they were: 2 and 4 Squadrons were equipped with the BE2 – the best plane at the time – but the others were a jumble of Blériots, Henri Farmans, Avros and Sopwith Tabloids (see page 25).

Eyewitness to Tragedy

Gathering a force like this was a new experience for everyone – and accidents were waiting to happen. On 12 August, as 3 Squadron prepared to take off from Netherhaven, a grumpy air mechanic looked on. James McCudden had joined the army as a boy bugler before transferring to the RFC in 1913. He was desperately keen to become a pilot and eager for any flying he could get.

James had been promised a lift in a two-seater

James McCudden, 1914

machine to Dover, but at the last minute his pilot had been ordered to take a single-seat plane. Now all he could do was look on dourly as the others had all the fun. He swung the prop for Lieutenant Robert Skene and his passenger, Air Mechanic Keith Barlow, and ducked under the wing to pull away the chocks. Skene trundled across the airfield and took off, disappearing behind one of the hangars. Then – SILENCE – the engine stopped. After what seemed an age James heard a noise like a distant clap of thunder.

He wrote later:

I ran for half a mile, and found the machine in a small copse of firs, so I got over the fence and pulled the wreckage away from the occupants and found them both dead . . . I shall never forget that morning at about half past six, kneeling by poor Keith Barlow and looking at the rising sun and then again at poor Barlow, who had no superficial injury and was killed purely by concussion, and wondering if it was going to be like this always.

James couldn't know the heartbreaking answer that August dawn would be 'yes'.

James McCudden became an air ace with 57 **kills** to his credit. Sadly, in 1918, three months after he was awarded the Victoria Cross, he died in an accident – when his engine stalled after take-off.

To France

On 13 August 1914 the British squadrons hopped across the Channel from Dover. The aircrew carried inflated car-tyre inner tubes to act as lifebelts if they ditched in the sea. Luckily nobody took the plunge, but one flyer impishly tried to drop his inner tube, like a fairground hoop, on to the top of the lighthouse at Cap Gris-Nez. After a 2-hour flight the British landed at Amiens. The first man on French soil was the high-spirited Lieutenant Hubert Harvey-Kelly. Just how high-spirited you'll find out shortly.

Following the aircraft as quickly as possible, the ground staff crossed to France in steam ships. The stores and heavy goods were loaded in a motley collection of civilian vehicles **commandeered** by the army –

Hubert Harvey-Kelly (on right) with a BE2a reconnaissance plane, August 1914

delivery lorries emblazoned with such slogans as LAZENBY'S SAUCE (THE WORLD'S APPETIZER), PEEK FREAN'S BISCUITS and STEPHENS' BLUE-BLACK INK. There was even a large van with the word BOVRIL painted in bold, black letters on it. Along the way the French people turned out to welcome the RFC. Air Mechanic James Gascoyne remembered:

> They assembled along the road and gave us terrific cheers and we were loaded up with wine, bottles of wine everywhere – the lorries had more wine than equipment I think! As a result I've never drunk wine since.

In the Path of the Hammer Blow

From their forward base at Maubeuge, the British aircraft were soon at work, spotting the movement of German troops. The first report, made on 19 August, was disappointing. If it had been the observer's homework, it would have scored 0/10!

> Did not pick my position on the map. Arrived at a big town, but could not place it on the map. On my return I discovered this to have been Brussels.

Thankfully the quality improved quickly. On 22 August machine after machine returned with alarming sightings of a vast enemy attack. Lieutenant Charles Rabagliati reported:

As soon as we got over our area, instead of seeing a few odd Germans I saw the whole area covered with hordes of field grey uniforms – advancing infantry, cavalry, transport and guns. In fact it looked as though the whole place was alive with Germans.

The sea of grey spotted by the awed lieutenant was the powerful German II Corps, which was about to slam into the BEF. The enemy had caught the British by surprise – and outnumbered them three to one. For a long, hard day the BEF held the Germans back in bitter street-fighting in the mining town of Mons. But the odds were so stacked against them that if the British did not retreat quickly they would be annihilated.

Retreat

On the evening of 23 August the British commander, Sir John French, weighed up the disturbing news given to him by the RFC. He didn't like it. In fact Sir John was one of those generals who wondered if aeroplanes weren't a new-fangled waste of time. But as report after report came in confirming the huge size of the German force, he decided to act. He cancelled plans for a counter-attack and ordered the BEF to pull out. He made the painful decision just in time.

In the blazing August heat, the BEF made a gallant fighting retreat – not knowing when or where it would end. The RFC abandoned their airfield at Maubeuge as

German shells pounded the site. Fuel and stores were set on fire, even as the planes took to the air. The ground crew piled into the lorries with essential equipment and set off down roads packed with soldiers and refugees.

Day after day the RFC pulled back with the army, flying from makeshift landing strips in fields of corn or, worse still, rutted fields of cabbages. This took a heavy toll on the delicate aircraft, with mechanics working though the night to repair shattered landing gear. Sometimes the ground crew had to pack up and run while the planes were in the air. Exhausted pilots returned from missions only to play a frustrating game of 'hunt the base'. One marker became a good luck symbol. The faithful Bovril lorry, with its large black letters, was unmistakable from the air.

Curious Combat

With ferocious fighting on the ground, it wasn't long before the airmen decided to join in. Pilots from both sides carried pistols, rifles and grenades, but during those first days of the war had done little more than annoy each other with them. On 25 August, however, two incidents showed that the conflict in the air was heating up too. The first was quite light-hearted.

Three BE2s from 2 Squadron were on patrol when they spotted a German Taube observing the French battle lines. The Taube, which means 'dove' in German, was a strange-looking plane, with wings shaped like those of a bird. It made a tempting target. Flight leader Lieutenant Hubert Harvey-Kelly dived into the attack. (Remember Hubert was described as 'high-spirited' — how about adding 'as mad as a hatter'!)

The bird-like Taube, designed by Austrian Igo Etrich

Determined to scare the life out of the enemy pilot, he brought the thrashing propeller of his BE2 to within 4 feet (1.25 m) of the tail of his victim. One small mistake and both planes would be spinning towards the hard earth. Joining in the sport, the other British pilots closed in on either side, while Hubert hung on behind.

The wretched German cursed the **Tommies** and tried to throw them off, but they stuck like glue. Worse, he could see they were cackling with laughter. Desperately, he landed in the nearest field and heaved a sigh of relief. Safe! Or maybe not . . . He glanced round to find the crazy

British landing beside him. Were they about to kill him?

Not surprisingly, he didn't wait to find out. Leaping from his plane, the German pilot sprinted towards nearby woods to hide. Imagine his horror when Hubert and the others noisily chased him, prowling through the undergrowth. After a few minutes' fruitless search, they gave up, set fire to the Taube and took off, leaving behind one very relieved enemy flyer.

Although this reads like a storyboard for an early Charlie Chaplin movie, it set a war record – the first victory in the air. And so far no one had been harmed. The second incident on that summer's day was far less innocent.

Lieutenant Rabagliati was patrolling at around 3–4,000 feet (925–1,230 m) when he came across a German plane. Both crews began to take potshots, Rabagliati with his Lee Enfield rifle, the German observer with a Mauser pistol, and neither pilot backed down. The lieutenant wrote later:

> We manoeuvred ourselves against one another.
> Sometimes we'd be extremely close, it seemed almost
> touching, other times we'd be out of range. We couldn't
> shoot through the propeller in front so we shot sideways.
> Not only was the other aeroplane going fast, but our own
> from which I was shooting was going fast. We fired a
> great many rounds – I fired over 100 – and then
> suddenly ... I saw the German pilot fall forward on to his
> joystick and the machine tipped and went down.

There was nothing of the silent film comedy in this encounter. A long war of kill or be killed had just begun in the air.

In those crazy August days the RFC came through its baptism of fire proudly. Like the soldiers they flew over, the airmen fell back in good order, leapfrogging from one makeshift airfield to another but always patrolling and reporting enemy movements. Crucially, British generals now had no doubts as to how useful the RFC had become. The early warning given to Sir John French had helped to save the BEF from extinction. And soon the time would come to turn and fight again . . .

FIGHTING FACTS

What Happened to the BEF?

The retreat from Mons is a proud episode in the history of the British Army. For 14 days the BEF made a fighting retreat and didn't break. It was tiny by European standards, but the soldiers were professionals. They could fire 15 rounds a minute from their Lee Enfield rifles and made the German **conscripts** pay a heavy price.

Finally the running came to an end on the River Marne and, together with the French, the BEF turned to launch a counter-attack. Now the Germans were driven back and both sides began a race to the sea in an effort to outflank each other. By October the rival armies had dug lines of trenches that stretched from the English Channel to Switzerland. This was the Western Front. Over the next four years the tiny British Army of 1914 grew to a force of over 4 million, able to slug it out with the Germans on equal terms. And as the army grew so did the RFC, from the few dozen planes of August 1914 to 22,647 aeroplanes and seaplanes by November 1918.

Gentlemen Only

So you reckon you are pilot material? Think you've got what it takes? Well, in 1914 your selection interview for the RFC might have gone something like this:

'How do you do? Take a seat. Right, Mr . . . Can you ride a horse? sail a boat? ride a motorcycle?

'Yes? Well done, you are just the type we want. With the skills you've learned from these sports – coordination, steady nerve, sense of balance – we'll have you flying solo in two hours.

'Now try this eyesight test. Can you pick out the different colours in this bundle of woollen strands? Red? Excellent! Green? Fine! Yellow? Marvellous!

'By the way, one last question, old chap. What's your background? Family and all that? Your father's a plumber? Oh dear! Sorry. Perhaps there might be a place for you in the infantry. We have standards to keep up, you know.'

In 1914 flying with the RFC was like becoming a member of an exclusive club for gentlemen. Most early recruits came from privileged backgrounds. One reason for this was money. Candidates were expected to pass the Royal Aero Club certificate of competence at their own expense, before they joined up. And this cost £70, at a time when a good wage for an ordinary worker was £3 a week.

By 1916 the supply of young men from public schools like Eton had begun to dry up. Reluctantly the RFC allowed working-class candidates like James McCudden and Edward 'Mick' Mannock (see pages 12–13) to train as pilots. Even so, older hands didn't like it and commented that the service had become 'quite a mixed bunch'. This wasn't meant as a compliment.

James McCudden

Earlier in this chapter you met James McCudden as a disgruntled air mechanic. For much of his career he was to stay disgruntled with the RFC and he became an **ace** the hard way. Repeated applications to become a pilot were turned down, but he was determined to gain experience. In 1915 he flew as an observer, fitting in the flying between his normal ground duties. In 1916 he was finally sent for pilot training and gained his 'wings' – his first-class pilot's certificate – on 30 May. He made his first kill on 6 September, bringing down a two-seater Albatros. By April 1918, when he was awarded the VC, he had shot down 54 enemy planes. The long citation commended his exceptional skill, noting:

> On two occasions, he totally destroyed four two-seater enemy aeroplanes on the same day, and on the last occasion all four machines were destroyed in the space of one hour and 30 minutes.

James added another three to his score before he was killed when his aircraft stalled after take-off on 9 July.
For more on aces turn to page 96.

Primitive Planes
To modern eyes the aircraft of 1914 look incredibly fragile.
- **Structure:** Most of the main parts were made from wood such as ash and spruce, braced with steel wires.
- **Skin:** The outer covering was made from fabric, often the finest Irish linen painted with acetone dope (varnish) to pull it taut and give it a smooth surface.
- **Cockpit:** The pilot sat on a seat made of wicker, often on top of the fuel tank. The RFC refused to fit armour plate to protect pilots from ground fire, even though the Germans soon began to do this.
- **Engines:** Most early British planes were powered by French rotary engines in which the cylinders whirled around a stationary shaft. Few aircraft had brakes. On the ground aeroplanes were held back by crewmen until the engine had built up enough revs for take-off.

- **Performance:** The average speed was about 60 mph (100 kph), with maximum heights ranging between 3,300 feet and 12,000 feet (950 and 3,500 m). While flight duration was good – most planes could stay in the air for 2 to 4 hours – the loads they could carry were still small. Even the weight of the pilot was crucial!

Don't Shoot! We're British!

One of the biggest problems facing RFC aircrew was the hail of rifle and machine-gun fire from the ground. Worse, it often came from BOTH sides. British soldiers were under orders not to shoot at aircraft unless they were certain they were German, but in practice they blazed away at anything that flew within range. The answer seemed to be clear: put markings on RFC planes – something that said, 'HOLD ON, WE'RE ON YOUR SIDE!' The enemy had already done this. The underside of every German aircraft was painted white with a large black cross on each wing.

At first the British tried painting their planes with a Union Jack, but this just looked like a smudge from the ground. The next idea was far more successful – the red, white and blue roundels still used by the RAF today. Although pilots nicknamed these 'the targets', fewer aircraft were shot down once they were given the new symbols.

Aircraft in the RFC, 1914

Type and country of origin	Crew and purpose	Speed	Weapons	Comments
Farman Longhorn – France	2 Reconnaissance & training	59 mph (94 kph) at sea level	None	Successful in its day. Flew a record distance of 350 miles (560 km) in 1910
Blériot XI – France	1 or 2 Reconnaissance	66 mph (105 km) at sea level	None	The RFC had 23 of these machines when the war began
BE2a – Britain	2 Reconnaissance	72 mph (115 kph) at 6,500 feet (2,000 m)	None at first, but the BE2c was armed with a **Lewis gun** by 1915	Designed by Geoffrey de Havilland, the BE2 was the first British aircraft to arrive in France
Avro 504 – Britain	2 Trainer	84 mph (134 kph) at sea level	None, but some were later fitted with Lewis guns for home-defence against Zeppelins or Gothas	Over 8,000 were made during the war, largely used to train pilots
Sopwith Tabloid – Britain	1 High-speed reconnaissance	$92^1/2$ mph (148 kph) at sea level	Usually none	Fitted with bomb racks by the Royal Naval Air Service, two Tabloids bombed Zeppelin sheds in October 1914

Aye-Aye! What's This?

Throughout the war reconnaissance remained the most important task of the RFC. The big battles would be won or lost on the ground and the generals needed all the information they could get. Only aircraft could probe beyond the German lines.

At first most observers were army officers, hastily scribbling notes or marking new features on maps. But the naked eye had its limitations. Sometimes it was difficult to notice small changes, such as a new machine-gun positions on a complex system of enemy trenches. Yet such tiny details could be crucial during an attack. What the army needed was a means of checking changes over time – in other words, they needed photographs!

A War of Lenses

The first British photos were taken during the Battle of the Aisne in 1915, using big, clumsy and heavy box cameras. The shots were taken though a hole cut in the floor of the plane. The problems were recalled by Lieutenant Archibald:

You yelled at the pilot when you were going to take a photograph so he kept the aircraft quite level and didn't tilt the angle of the camera . . . It was a difficult job, because first you had to look through the hole to see the target you were photographing. Then you lost sight of it as you put the camera between your knees and pressed the trigger. I became rather the star photographer, being very small and able to bend down to adjust the camera.

By 1916 techniques had improved so much that a picture taken from 15,000 feet (4,500 m) could be magnified to show the footprints of an infantryman. In the last two years of the war the British alone took more than half a million reconnaissance photos.

The Dying Aviator

This song, with its black humour, soon
became an RFC favourite

A handsome young airman lay dying
Lay dying. (Chorus)
And as on the aerodrome he lay.
He lay.
To the mechanics who came round him
   sighing.
Came sighing.
These last dying words he did say.
He did say.
'Take the cylinder out of my kidneys.
Of his kidneys.
The connecting rod out of my brain.
Of his brain.
From the small of my back take the camshaft
His back
And assemble the engine again.'

(Again.)

Anon.

A STRANGE AFFAIR WITH A MACHINE GUN

BATTLE BRIEFING

By the end of November 1914 the war on the ground had reached stalemate. As the troops dug in, generals on both sides looked to their air forces to give them an edge. Britain rushed ahead with plans to expand the RFC, training more pilots and observers, and also the small army of men needed to keep them in the air — armourers, fitters, mechanics and riggers. By May 1915 2,260 new aircraft were on order.

Ideas about war in the air were changing quickly too. In August 1914 RFC Staff Officer Sykes had said, 'There should be no attempt at aerial conflict', and the Germans agreed with him. Yet by the spring of 1915 both sides had developed 'scouts' — fighting aircraft designed to shoot down enemy planes and protect their own reconnaissance flights.

Ominously, these scouts were armed not just with rifles or pistols – they carried machine guns.

On the British side, one of the pioneers of this lethal technology was Lieutenant Louis Strange. In 1915 he was to experience one of the most bizarre episodes of the war.

AERIAL ATHLETICS

A Horse of Course

Louis was a Dorset farmer and a very good horseman. He was never happier than when out with the local hunt. Nothing could beat a good gallop across the countryside: the cry of the hounds, the charging horsemen, the joy of the chase. It was a wonderful English tradition that sorted the men from the boys!

One exhilarating chase found him in the saddle for an hour and 40 minutes. Flushed with excitement, he leapt every barrier in his path – gates, hedges and ditches flying by. At the end he was the only rider still up with the hounds. For a countryman, it was a memory to treasure.

Horses were Louis's greatest love – until he saw his first aeroplane at the army **manoeuvres** in September 1912. Like many keen horsemen, Louis was a part-time soldier in the Dorset Yeomanry – a unit of volunteer cavalry. The Dorset troopers attended the manoeuvres every year to sharpen their skills, but that September there was a novelty: the newly formed RFC joined in too.

Learning New Lessons

As the planes buzzed and wheeled overhead, most soldiers dismissed them as thrilling but useless toys. What good were they compared to a dashing troop of cavalry? But Louis wasn't so sure ...

In the manoeuvres, the army divided into two teams, each led by a general determined to outfox his opponent. Sir James Grierson, the commander of Blue Team, was up against Sir Douglas Haig, the leader of Red Team. Each side was supported by seven RFC aeroplanes and an airship. In the opinion of most, Grierson was the underdog – a plodder – but on the day he made better use of his flyers.

As each side took position, one of Blue Team's planes spotted Red troops deploying for a mass attack. At once the crew flew back to HQ to report, only to find Grierson downcast by their news. He had already sent his cavalry in the wrong direction – the war games were lost before the fighting had begun. At once the airmen stepped into the breach. They flew new orders to the Blue cavalry, who neatly turned round and chopped off the Red advance. Grierson realized he had glimpsed the future.

*

The impression left on my mind is that their use has revolutionized the art of war. So long as hostile aircraft are hovering over one's troops all movements are liable to be seen and reported, and therefore the first step in war will be to get rid of the hostile aircraft.

Sadly, Grierson's opinions were ignored and the same lessons had to be learned again in 1914–15.

Back in Dorset, the yeomanry had long and loud arguments as the beer flowed after training sessions. Most troopers stayed faithful to the horse. In the next war, they argued, cavalry would be the decisive weapon. What could beat the massed charge of horses and the cold steel of the sabre?

But Louis knew that times were changing. He agreed with Grierson. 'Since that Blériot chap flew the Channel without falling into it, Britain is no longer an island,' he declared. 'Mark my words, within a few years aeroplanes will replace cavalry.'

As glasses were drained, and drained again, Louis issued his challenge. He would learn to fly . . . and what's more he would swoop over the Dorset Yeomanry at the manoeuvres in 1914. The bet was eagerly taken on all sides.

Flight School

Louis joined the RFC in 1913 and took his first lessons at the new Central Flying School at Upavon Downs on Salisbury Plain. The aeroplanes and the flight instructors were a motley collection of men and machines, mostly brought in from France.

One instructor, Louis Noel, always gave a blunt speech to his perky pupils before their first solo flight:

I have told you how to fly. Have you understood? Yes? Well, I give you the last chance to say no ... Very well, you can fly, do you hear? I, Louis Noel, say you can fly. I speak no more. I go to the bar. If you commit suicide that is bad, but if you almost do that it will be much the worse for you.

Noel went on to become a French ace.

Fortunately, it was quite hard to be killed in the underpowered and slow machines of the time. They were little more than powered gliders with large areas of canvas and wood to absorb the shock of a crash. For new pupils, flying was limited to early mornings or late evenings – or other times when there was little wind. A training aircraft usually had no cockpit, just a seat for the instructor and a perch behind his back for the trainee.

Louis later recalled his early lessons with some amusement:

We knew nothing of the dual-control method of instruction. The pupil sat behind the instructor and could reach over his shoulder and use the control stick. There was, however, no way for the pupil to get his legs into contact with the rudder bar.

A student and instructor in a biplane

After a few lessons instructor and pupil changed places. Louis earned his pilot's licence in three weeks without any accidents.

With a Machine Gun to France

Louis went on to become a proficient flyer and was assigned as a lieutenant to 5 Squadron. On 1 May 1914 he took part in a daring new RFC training exercise – a bomb-dropping competition. Already a few flyers believed their planes could join in rather than just observe the fighting on the ground. From 300 feet (90 m) Louis's tiny bombs landed in a spread that averaged only $25^{1}/4$ feet (8 m) from the centre of the target. Remarkable! It was close enough to win the competition, but not to impress watching army officers.

Planes carrying bombs? A waste of time, they argued. Yes, some aircraft hit the target, but conditions were perfect. What would happen if they were being shot at? What about bad weather? And look at the payload — so small as to be worthless.

When the war began, the RFC was still under strict orders to observe and report, not to fight. Louis, however, wasn't put off. He already had another bee in his bonnet: he wanted to fit a machine gun in his plane.

It sounded a preposterous idea. A gun and ammunition would be a heavy load, perhaps too heavy. The recoil (the kickback when the gun was fired) meant the weapon had to be fastened to the aircraft structure or it would fly out of the hands of the gunner. More difficult still, it had to be fired through the web of struts and wires that held the plane together. There was a running joke among pilots that not even a bird could fly through this maze. So what chance of blasting away with a stream of bullets without bringing the whole blooming thing down? But Louis was determined. While his **CO** turned a quizzical blind eye, he strapped a Lewis gun to his aircraft, a Maurice Farman 'Loghorn'.

Louis had little time to practise with his new weapon before war broke out. And more annoying still, when the RFC flew to France (see page 14) he was left behind. For three days irritating delays left him hopping with frustration on the ground. And then he was lumbered with a passenger who turned the cross-Channel flight

The Maurice Farman S7 Longhorn

into a mini-adventure. The man, a transport driver, was drunk – and heavy.

When Louis finally took off for Amiens on 16 August his underpowered plane was ridiculously full. The groaning Farman carried:

- pilot . . . and full kit
- 13-stone (83 kg) passenger . . . and full kit
- machine gun . . . and ammunition.

The aircraft **cut daisies** for a long time before it finally clawed into the air. After a 2^1/2-hour flight through torrential rain, Louis landed, and his plane was surrounded by a cheering French crowd. Graciously, and unsteadily, the transport driver stood up and waved back – with an empty whisky bottle.

Too Slow

On 22 August, just before the enemy sledgehammer hit the BEF, a cheeky German flyer in an Albatros biplane decided to tweak the nose of the RFC. And it worked. As he flew 4,000 feet (1,230 m) over their airfield at Maubeuge the intruder stirred up a hornet's nest. Outraged British pilots grabbed an assortment of rifles, pistols and hand grenades and ran to their planes. If they could catch 'the **Hun**' they intended to bring him down.

Louis set off as eagerly as the rest. Was this the day the machine gun would prove its worth? Well, no. He soon lagged far behind the others, the weight of the gun proving too much for the Farman in a climb. He wrote:

> I set off with Lt. Penn Gaskell to work the Lewis gun. The enemy machine made off while we were still climbing over our aerodrome, and I imagine its occupants must have enjoyed a good laugh at our futile efforts.

But bad news was in store when he landed. Louis's CO ordered him to unship the gun and its mounting and make do with a rifle. Then at least he might be able to catch the enemy sometimes.

Getting Rid of Hostile Aircraft

In the following months Sir James Grierson's 1912 prediction came true. A few enterprising pilots took the lead in equipping their aircraft to enable them to shoot down German planes. If the skies were cleared of enemy reconnaissance flights, they argued, the German Army would be blinded.

As the action hotted up, Louis complained long and loud about his impounded machine gun. His mission reports summed up the problem. On 15 October, flying a two-man Avro, he chased and caught an enemy Aviatik. His observer blasted away with a rifle, but the chances of doing any damage while firing in an 80-mph (130 kph) slipstream were slim. Over 70 bullets later, with no hits, they saw the German duck into a cloud and escape, unharmed.

Finally Louis won his argument and was allowed to experiment with a machine gun again. The Avro was a **tractor** plane, not a pusher like the Farman. This meant the propeller was in the way, so the Lewis gun could fire only sideways and behind. Even so, it soon paid off. On 22 November, as Louis was returning to base, he spotted another Aviatik. This time he had the advantage of height and dived to attack.

As they zoomed across the bows of the enemy plane, Louis's observer, Lieutenant Small, let fly with a broadside and then another long burst as Louis closed in again. The German pilot **put on rudder** and slipped to one side, letting his observer, a Prussian guard officer, return fire with a pistol. Then . . . CLACK, CLACK . . . CLACK . . . the Lewis gun was empty. Great timing!

Hastily – which wasn't all that hasty, with hands encumbered by thick flying gloves – Lieutenant Small changed the **drum** and opened fire again. Immediately the Aviatik fell away on one wing as the pilot dived steeply to escape. Around 20 machine-gun bullets had just peppered the instrument panel inches in front of his face. He wanted out and was almost over German lines and safe. But Louis was in no mood to let him go. He followed the Aviatik down and cut in front of it, less than 1,500 feet (460 m) from the enemy's trenches. At that moment a plume of black smoke came from the Aviatik's engine and the plane lumbered down to land in a field in the British reserve lines.

Machine-gun Athletics

Louis was at the start of a lethal race. By the summer of 1915 French, Germans and British were all flying fighter aircraft fitted with machine guns. But the technology was still unreliable – as he was about to find out.

Louis now joined 6 Squadron as flight leader and, because of his experience, had the pick of a mixed bag of aircraft. His choice was the first single-seat, tractor biplane assigned to the unit, a Martinsyde Scout. As planes went, it had all the flying ability of a pig. It was slow, unstable and sluggish in responding to the controls. What it did have, though, was a Lewis gun fitted to a fixed mounting on top of the upper wing – so it fired over the propeller. Louis was happy.

On 10 May he was on patrol behind German lines when he caught sight of an Aviatik well above him. At a painful 60 mph (100 kph), the best the Martinsyde could do, he climbed in pursuit. So far so good, until the enemy observer glanced down and warned the pilot that a British plane was closing in. Now a race was on and the Aviatik slowly began to pull away.

At around 8,500 feet (2,600 m) the Martinsyde reached its **ceiling** and Louis knew his prey would be out of reach in seconds. Pulling the **joystick** back to lift the nose, he fired a long burst that emptied the Lewis gun. And missed. Cursing, he watched the Aviatik fly peacefully on – undamaged.

When Louis calmed down he began to realize he was in a risky position. He'd flown a long way into enemy skies and the defenceless Martinsyde made a tempting target. Time to turn for home. Time to change the ammo drum. Time for the most terrifying moments of his life …

Louis's thoughts ran at lightning speed: 'The Lewis gun is on top of the upper wing … Hold the joystick between knees … Stretch up to unclip the drum. One quick twist and … Damn … Stuck. Assess situation: in a gentle dive back to Allied lines … about 20 miles away … Air speed about 75 mph. OK. Try again. Gloves off for a better grip. Stand up this time … Good grasp … HEAVE … HEAVE. Oh no! Plane's almost at stalling speed … Port wing has dropped … Losing balance … Fallen against joystick … Full left rudder … Going into a spin … Safety belt has come loose … Hold on!'

To Louis's horror, the plane rolled over and pointed its undercarriage at the sky. He was left dangling underneath, like a circus trapeze artist, but here there was no safety net. All that stopped him plummeting to earth was his vice-like grip on the ammo drum. And all that stopped the drum coming loose was a 6-mm crossed thread of low-tensile steel.

Louis wrote later:

Only a few seconds before I had been cursing because I could not get the drum off. Now I prayed fervently that it would stay on for ever.

If the drum came loose he was dead.

Louis Strange dangling upside down from his plane

For how long could you hold your weight, hanging from a bar in a gym? For how long could you hold on to a slowly spinning, upside-down biplane? A spin that was making you sick with dizziness?

Exactly! Now think about Louis's plight for a head-spinning second!

Louis knew he had to act fast. Letting go with one hand, he reached back and made a blind grab for a wing strut. This left him hanging momentarily from the drum by one hand. (Now try that in the gym!) Once he had a good grip on the strut, he began a series of swinging kicks to lever his legs into the cockpit. On the third attempt he hooked one foot in, then the other, booted the joystick to **jam on full aileron and rudder**. . . and flopped into the cockpit as the Martinsyde righted itself.

Danger Over? No!

The plane was in a roaring dive towards the Belgian town of Menin and had fallen almost 7,000 feet (2,150 m). Struggling against gravity, Louis managed to push his feet on to the rudder controls, correct the spin and level out.

Shaken to the core, he flew back to base – and sheepishly stayed quiet about the incident. He didn't want to be a laughing stock for weeks. This had two weird results.

- *Weird result one*: He was put on a charge by his commanding officer for damaging his seat and instruments by kicking them. Unfair or what?

- **Weird result two**: The crew of the German Avaitik claimed a victory. They had *seen* the British plane turn over and the pilot fall out. But there was no wreckage to back their claim ... and no one would believe their story.

FIGHTING FACTS

'Let Me Report Him'

Remember the Aviatik brought down by Louis on 22 November 1914? The British infantrymen who captured the German flyers passed on a hilarious tale.

- The pilot had landed because he was terrified. But, although the engine was damaged, it would have made it back to German lines.
- The Prussian officer/observer thought they had landed because the pilot was injured. He was furious when he found out what had really happened.
- The Prussian threw aside the British soldiers and started to beat up the pilot. When he was held back he cried out in anguish: 'Let me report this coward to German flying headquarters.'

The Race for the Machine Gun

In spite of the efforts of British pilots like Louis, it was the French who led the way in air warfare. On 5

October 1914 an observer called Louis Quenault shot down an Aviatik with a Hotchkiss machine gun. The French plane was a rear-engined Voisin so, unlike in Louis's two-man Avro, mounting a machine gun that could fire forward wasn't a problem. By February 1915 the French had around 50 pushers equipped with similar guns.

But a far more important breakthrough was already being tested. In December 1914 the French pilot Roland Garros visited the workshops of plane builder Raymond Saulnier. Roland was a famous stunt flyer before the war, setting a world record for high flying of an astonishing 18,000 feet (5,500 m). He came to Raymond with a complaint. So far, he had been unable to shoot down any Germans:

> When I was able to outmanoeuvre my adversary, my observer never succeeded in shooting him down with a light rifle.

What he wanted was a device that would allow him to fire a fixed, forward-mounted machine gun through his own whirling airscrew and not blast off the propeller blades. This meant that as he manoeuvred his plane, he also aimed his own weapon. Could Saulnier suggest an answer? Working together, the two men came up with a simple solution: deflector plates. They worked out that only about 7 per cent of the bullets would hit the propeller blades, so why not bounce them out of the way?

Sounds like a crazy idea? It was. If the bullets bounced off the plates in the wrong direction, the pilot could shoot down his own plane. But, although it was crude, it worked. Roland used his own Morane monoplane for the experiments and in April 1915 brought down five enemy planes in two weeks. That summer Allied pilots in Moranes fitted with deflector plates ruled the sky – but theirs was a short-lived joy.

Fokker Fodder

On 18 April Roland was flying low over German lines – too low – when a single bullet fired from the ground cut his fuel line. The engine died and he had no choice but to land behind enemy lines. Desperately, he tried to burn the Morane to protect its secrets, but he was too slow. Troops arrived and captured the precious plane. Roland was heartbroken – he had helped to develop a battle-winning weapon, only to hand it over to the Germans.

They, of course, were jubilant. So this was the mystery plane that was doing so much damage! The Morane was dismantled and the gun, engine and propeller were given to Anthony Fokker, a brilliant Dutch aircraft designer working in Germany. And with them came a personal message from the head of the German air force, Oberstleutnant Hermann von der Lieth-Thomsen: could he produce a forward-firing machine gun as good or better than this?

Remarkably, Fokker's team came up with an answer in

a few days. They had already designed a monoplane scout similar to the Morane – the Fokker E1. Made of welded steel tubes instead of wood, it was light and fast. Now they armed it with the first synchronized machine gun. Instead of the propeller stopping the bullets, it was connected to the gun by a pushrod control mechanism. When the trigger was pressed an even spread of bullets flew between the blades without striking them.

Improved Fokker EIIs were delivered to German frontline units during the summer of 1915. The plane was to make two fearsome aces: Oswald Boelcke and Max Immelman. By early 1916 Allied pilots felt they were little more than 'Fokker fodder'. Even RFC HQ seemed to be admitting defeat when it issued a rather desperate order:

The Fokker EI, 1915

> *Until the Royal Flying Corps are in possession of a*
> *machine as good or better than the German Fokker ...*
> *it must be laid down as a hard and fast rule that a*
> *machine proceeding on reconnaissance must be*
> *escorted by at least three fighting machines.*

Fokker Foiled

In 1916 the MP Pemberton Billing caused an outrage in the House of Commons when he deplored the poor quality of British aircraft:

> *Every one of our pilots at the front knows when he*
> *steps into them that if he gets back it will be more by*
> *luck and his skill than any mechanical assistance that*
> *he will get from the people who provide him with the*
> *machines ... I would suggest that quite a number of*
> *officers in the RFC have been murdered rather than*
> *killed.*

Strong stuff. But even as he spoke a new generation of aircraft was tipping the balance against the Fokker.

Fokker Stopper 1

The DH2, designed by Geoffrey de Havilland, was a pusher biplane. It looked painfully obsolete but, despite having a rear-mounted engine, it was a proper single-seat scout. With a speed of 85 mph (140 kph) at 7,000 feet 2,150 m), and a ceiling of 14,000 feet (4,300 m), the DH2 could outperform the Fokker – just. The pilot had a clear view in front of him and a fixed, forward-mounted machine gun.

Fokker Stopper 2

The French Nieuport Scout looked to the future with a front-mounted engine. It had a top speed of 107 mph (170 kph) and a ceiling of 17,400 feet (5,350 m). It was armed with a Lewis gun on top of the wing, firing safely over the propeller. It became the favourite plane of two top British aces, Albert Ball and James McCudden.

Fokker Stopper 3

Finally, in May 1916, the RFC began to receive the first British plane with a forward-mounted machine gun and an interrupter gear to fire through the propeller: the Sopwith 1^1/$_2$ Strutter.

During the summer of 1916 the RFC regained command of the air, but it was a narrow lead that was soon to be challenged by a new generation of German aircraft.

RFC Aircraft

Type and country of origin	Crew and purpose	Speed	Weapons	Comments
Martinsyde S.I Britain	1 Fighter	87 mph (139 km) at sea level	One Lewis gun	A poor plane, withdrawn from service by mid-1915
Morane-Saulnier France	1 or 2 Fighter	71 mph (114 kph) at sea level	One fixed Lewis gun firing through the propeller	One of the first planes used for aerial combat
Nieuport 11 France I	1 Fighter	97 mph (155 kph) at sea level	One fixed, forward firing Lewis gun, mounted above the upper wing	Nicknamed the Bébé (Baby), this was a highly manoeuvrable plane with a fast rate of climb
Sopwith 1½ Strutter Britain	2 Fighter, bomber and reconnaissance	106 mph (170 kph) at sea level	One fixed, forward-firing Vickers machine gun, one free-firing Lewis gun and up to 130 lb (59 kg) of bombs	A very successful fighter until it was outclassed by the German Albatros

German Aircraft

Type and country of origin	Crew and purpose	Speed	Weapons	Comments
Aviatik B and C Germany	2 Reconnaissance	89 mph (142 kph) at sea level	At first unarmed, the C.I was equipped with one forward-firing Parabellum machine gun	A successful plane in widespread use 1914–17
Etrich Taube Austria-Hungary and Germany	2 Reconnaissance and training	71 mph (142 kph) at sea level	None	A striking aircraft with a bird-like structure. Over 500 were built and the Taube stayed in service until 1916
Fokker EI Germany	1 Fighter	87 mph (139 kph) at sea level	One fixed, forward-firing machine gun	The plane that shocked the Allies in the summer of 1915. Pilots did not expect to be shot at by a plane approaching from behind

On the Wings of the Morning

A sudden roar, a mighty rushing sound,
a jolt or two, a smoothly sliding rise,
a tumbled blur of disappearing ground,
and all sense of motion slowly dies.
Quiet and calm the earth slips past below,
as underneath a bridge still waters flow.

My turning wing inclines towards the ground;
The ground itself glides up with graceful swing
and at the plane's far tip twirls slowly round,
then drops from sight again beneath the wing
to slip away serenely as before,
a cubist patterned carpet on the floor.

Hills gently sink and valleys gently fill.
The flattened fields grow ludicrously small;
slowly they pass underneath and slower still
until they hardly seem to move at all.
Then suddenly they disappear from sight,
hidden by fleeting wisps of faded white.

The wing-tips, faint and dripping, dimly show,
blurred by wreaths of mist that intervene.
Weird half-seen shadows flicker to and fro
across the pallid fog-bank's blinding screen.
At last the choking mists release their hold,
and all the world is silver, blue and gold.

Jeffrey Day

Note: Jeffrey flew for the Royal Navy Air Service. On 27 February 1918
he took on six enemy planes single-handed and was shot down and
killed.

AIRSHIP
KILLER

BATTLE BRIEFING

Aircraft were not the only way to take to the skies. Before the war, lighter-than-air technology seemed far more promising – and the Germans were the world leaders. By 1914, airships were gigantic yet graceful machines able to carry tons of cargo – or bombs – at a time when aircraft struggled to take off with one or two people. They had a range of over 1,000 miles (1,600 km), a speed of around 50–60 mph (80–96 kph) and an operational ceiling of about 13,000 feet (14,000 m). Crew quarters and engines were suspended from the framework while the huge bags of hydrogen gas, called balloonets, were carried inside. Hydrogen, a lighter-than-air gas, gave the airships their lift, but it was highly flammable.

The Death of New York

When the war began the British expected an immediate attack by enemy airships. For years there had been scare stories about the destruction that would rain from the skies. The top science-fiction writer H. G. Wells wrote a best-selling serial called The War in the Air. In this cracking adventure, a fleet of airships cross the Atlantic to destroy New York and smash the city, leaving it in ruins with many people dead.

Fuelled by fears like these, there was a spate of airship sightings and wild rumours of German spies. Something had to be done to reassure the public, but by September 1914 the RFC was busy in Europe. After some squabbling between the army and the navy, the air defence of Britain was handed over to the Royal Naval Air Service (RNAS).

Winston Churchill, then First Lord of the Admiralty (head of the navy), laid down the key features of a defence scheme:

- Anti-aircraft guns and searchlights were to protect key targets such as oil depots and docks.
- Interceptor squadrons of aircraft were to be based on the French and Belgian coasts to catch enemy airships before they reached Britain.
- London would be defended by a squadron of aeroplanes based at Hendon.
- Ordinary people must be given guidance about what to expect and police and fire brigades prepared. Plans must be made to turn off city lights.

Punch cartoon showing John Bull (Britain) giving German Zepplin a withering look
Zepplin (as 'The Fat Boy'): I wants to make your flesh creep.
John Bull: Right-o!

Slow in Coming

If the British were worried, the Germans were keen not to disappoint them. But they had problems. As often happens, speculation was far ahead of the facts. By August 1914 the German Army only had seven airships and three of these were soon shot down by ground fire over the battlefields of Belgium and France. The German Navy was even worse off. Out of three airships, two had accidentally gone up in flames, while the third had to be kept ready to support the High Seas fleet in any clash with the Royal Navy. It took months to build nine new Zeppelins ... but then the time to strike arrived.

WILD HAWK

First Strike

The first airship raid on England came on 19 January 1915. Three German Navy Zeppelins, L3, L4 and L6, set out for East Anglia on a night attack. L6 had to turn back with engine trouble, but the others flew on. They reached the Norfolk coast and dropped their bombs on Yarmouth before pushing inland to hit King's Lynn. Neither town had any important military targets and both were poorly defended against attack from the air. Four civilians were killed and a handful of homes destroyed.

The nation was shocked, but puzzled too. What on earth were these monsters after? The only sensible answer seemed too horrible. Surely, the papers argued, they must have been stalking the King and Queen. The royal estate at Sandringham was not far away and the royal family had only returned to London the day before. Had the Kaiser, the German emperor, stooped to this – sending airships by night to assassinate his cousins at their country home, where he had been a welcome guest before the war? True or not, it seemed like another German outrage!

The Times was to declare that this attack had brought to an end 'the age-long immunity of the heart of the British Empire from the sight of a foe and the sound of an enemy missile'. It also brought angry public demands for action. There had been lighting controls in London since

A Zeppelin (L32) in flight

the war began but the towns of East Anglia were brightly lit on that dark, winter night. Belatedly, the blackout was now extended across the South and the Midlands.

Worse, there were too few anti-aircraft guns to defend every potential target. In an unseemly hurry, a mobile force of lorries carrying machine guns, pom-poms and searchlights was formed. If the Zeppelins were spotted in time, perhaps by ships in the Channel or observers along the coast, these airship hunters would rush to block their path.

Target London

Yet, in spite of these precautions, the raids continued. The 'Zepps' seemed to move across the skies of England at will, and on 31 May 1915 London was attacked for the first time. LZ38 crossed the Channel and reached Stoke Newington, north-east London, before it was spotted at 23:20. As the airship soared over east London the crew dropped grenades and incendiary (fire) bombs on the houses below.

Once again, innocent civilians were the victims. Mrs C. Smith, living in Cowper Street, recalled:

I had just got into bed when I heard a terrible rushing of wind and shouts of 'Fire' and 'The Germans are here'. I jumped out of bed and carried my four children into the basement and then went out to the street door and saw the house next door was on fire and people were

helping to get the children out. The father was burnt
and the daughter, who my daughter used to play with,
had met her death … We later found the poor little dear
had crawled under the bed to get away from the flames.

LZ38 had dropped 3,000 lb (1,360 kg) of bombs, killed seven people and injured 35. More significantly, it had terrified the population of London. The Zeppelins looked deadly and sinister – like giant alien spacecraft might appear today. While their tiny payload could inflict only limited damage, they seemed far more dangerous to the people of a frightened city.

The little girl who died was called Elsie Leggett. Shortly afterwards, her sister Mary also died of her injuries. Grimly fascinated, thousands of Londoners paid a penny to walk through the remains of their home. Many must have wondered if they would be next – and they wanted revenge.

A Problem Pilot

On 7 May 1915 Lieutenant Reginald Warneford was posted to I Wing Royal Navy Air Service (see pages 67–8) The wing was stationed at St Pol airfield, near Dunkirk in France – the front line of England's air defence. The plan was simple: catch the Zepps leaving or returning to their bases in German-occupied Belgium. It was easier ordered than done.

The commander at St Pol was Arthur Longmore and he

was not the happiest of men. His new pilot was a rebel. He glanced down Warneford's record again and sighed.

Born in 1891 in India, the son of a civil engineer. Joined the merchant navy as a boy of 13. An officer in the Indian Steam Navigation Company when the war began. Volunteered for the Royal Navy Air Service in 1915. Stubborn . . . easily bored . . . irked by discipline . . . undoubtedly brave . . . As wild as a hawk.

Reginald Warneford

In a firm interview Longmore warned Reginald that he came to France with an 'unsavoury' reputation. 'I'll be keeping an eye on you, Warneford,' he said sternly. But, he continued in a more kindly tone, 'Think on it. This time you have a chance to start again. I will judge you solely on your behaviour in 1 Wing.' It seemed the advice fell on deaf ears. Only hours later Reginald was back in his office for a severe ticking-off. The Lieutenant had recklessly driven one of the airfield's few motor tenders into a ditch. Longmore later wrote:

He was one of the most astounding characters I ever
met. Here was a case of a man who knew absolutely
no fear, and my problem was to keep him alive as long
as possible and use him to do the maximum damage
against the Germans.

But sadly, 'as long as possible' didn't turn out to be that
long . . .

Fighting Mad

The next day Reginald more than made up for his
mistakes, dragging his unfortunate observer, John
D'Albiac, with him! They were patrolling between
Zeebrugge and Ostend when Reginald spotted a
German reconnaissance plane and set off in pursuit. The
enemy machine tried to lose him, skimming away at little
more than rooftop height. Reginald was overjoyed – a
challenge! Flying and firing his rifle at the same time, he
chased the German plane back to base in Ostend,
forcing the terrified crew to land.

When they got back to the RFC base John was
fuming. The fuel tank was almost empty – in a few
minutes they would have had to make an emergency
landing. He complained to the CO that Reginald had
ignored his signals that they were running out of petrol
and put them both in peril with his wild heroics. He
never wanted to be teemed up with 'this madman' again.

In the coming weeks Reginald was equally unstoppable,

attacking any German aircraft that came along and bombing troop and gun positions. Longmore was impressed and decided to give Reginald 'free rein' to seek his own targets. Better still, the commander got hold of the best weapon he could for his 'wild hawk' – a Morane Saulnier monoplane. This single-seater French aircraft had deflector plates fitted to the propellers (see pages 44–5) and Reginald was one of the first British pilots to be given a crack at the new plane.

The Death of L37

On the evening of 6 June 1915 Longmore received a message from the Admiralty: three airships that had just attacked England were returning to base. At once he ordered two pilots from I Wing to bomb the airship sheds at Evere in Belgium, while Reginald was sent up to see what he could find. He took off at 01:00 on 7 June, his Morane Saulnier loaded with six 20-lb (9-kg) bombs strapped under the fuselage.

That short summer night Reginald's luck was in. He had only been in the air a few minutes when he caught sight of his prey. In the far distance was a German Army airship. Later he learned that this was LZ37, commanded by Oberleutnant von der Haegen, with a crew of 28 on board. LZ37 had set out on a night raid with two other airships but they had all turned back due to poor weather. More surprisingly, LZ37 was not one of the airships the Admiralty had mentioned – Reginald ran into the lone airship by pure chance.

At first it seemed that the Zepp would get away. It took Reginald 45 minutes of hard flying to catch up with his giant opponent. It was 01:50, somewhere near Bruges, when they began their David and Goliath battle in the air. Reginald closed in but was met by a blast of machine-gun fire and banked away, trying to gain height. As he wheeled aside von der Haegen swung the nose of the airship after him. It turned into a game of cat and mouse as the German gunners tried to swat the buzzing aircraft, while Reginald tried to climb out of range.

For 20 minutes the opponents manoeuvred in the dark, then abruptly LZ37 stopped firing and turned

Reginald Warneford attacking a Zeppelin

towards base. Perhaps von der Haegen felt the enemy pilot had tried his best and was not a real threat. He was wrong!

Reginald had slowly climbed to 11,000 feet (3,400 m) and, switching off his engine, dived to the attack. At 7,000 feet (2,150 m) and barely 150 feet (45 m) above the enemy, he began his bombing run. Coming in from the stern, he skimmed the length of the airship with no effect. Were his bombs duds? But as the sixth and last was released, an explosion tore across the forward section of LZ37.

The next moments were like a vision of hell. The stricken Zeppelin began to disintegrate in mid-air. Burning hydrogen gas belched into the night, like an erupting volcano. In 6 seconds the broken hulk of the airship plunged to the ground, raining a fearsome litter of smashed framework and burning fabric.

The Human Cost

Slung underneath their ship in two control cars, the crew realized the ship was on fire. Some leapt into the air to escape the flames, while others clung on frantically. Tragically LZ37 did not fall into open fields. The wreckage crashed on to a convent in the suburbs of Ghent. Two nuns, a man and a child were killed, while others were seriously injured.

Yet amazingly one crewman survived. Arthur Muhler, the ship's coxswain (he steered the airship), fell through the roof of the convent and landed in a bed. He escaped with burns, bruising and shock – and a harrowing tale:

> The men in the forward control car were the first to feel the great shudder of the explosion. Above us the vast envelope quivered and began to wrinkle and collapse. The wheel went dead in my hands and the gondola trembled. All around were shouts and confused orders. I saw dark shapes of men silhouetted against a ruddy glow, their flailing hands trying to protect their faces. Some of them climbed over the sides of the car and flung themselves into space. I could not make myself let go of the wheel. I clung to it like a drowning man until it broke in my hands. I was flung to the floor. The scorching heat increased and increased and our clothes burst into flames. The gondola began to tilt and rock until, with a terrible sound of breaking wood and metal, it tore away from the main structure and plunged towards the ground. I knew no more until I woke up in hospital.

As the airship blew up, Reginald's joy was short-lived. His plane was caught in the blast, flipped on its back and hurtled upwards for 200 feet (60 m). It wasn't until the Morane dropped into a nosedive that the controls finally responded. But the danger was far from over. Reginald couldn't restart the engine and he was over enemy-occupied territory. There was nothing for it but to try an emergency landing.

He landed in a field next to a farmhouse and put his hand on his revolver. Surely, with the sky lit up brighter than Blackpool illuminations, the area would be crawling with troops? Frantically Reginald inspected his engine and found that a fuel feed line from the rear tank to the pump had split. It took 15 heart-stopping minutes to complete running repairs, but there was another more basic problem. It usually took two men to start a plane. In his report he recalled his frantic take-off:

*Without another chap I could not keep the engine running long enough for me to get back into the cockpit – I was pretty desperate by then. I pulled and pushed and bounced her along until I got her nose pointing down a steep hill. Then I swung the prop. I kept on hauling and pushing – she started to move slowly at first and then as she gathered speed I knew she wouldn't stop. I made a leap for the cockpit just as the **Boche** charged out of the wood firing in my direction.*

Yet Reginald was still not safe. The weather had worsened and now thick mist and fog were hiding the ground. Unable to get his bearings, he headed south-west. With no idea where he was and with fuel running out, the tired pilot had to play a dangerous game. From time to time he dropped into the fog, almost hugging the ground, to look for landmarks. Finally, his petrol exhausted, he landed on the sands at Cap Gris-Nez to wait for daylight. When the sun came up he was refuelled by a French unit and returned to St Pol at 10:30.

Warneford, VC

Within days Reginald had become a national hero. For the first time an airship had been shot down by an aeroplane. He received a telegraph from the Admiralty, carrying the personal congratulations of King George V, and the stunning news that he was to be awarded the Victoria Cross. On 9 June the French government announced that he was to be made a Chevalier de Legion d'Honneur.

Commander Longmore was delighted. His faith in Reginald had been justified, and of course this was a feather in the cap of the whole RNAS. Proudly he gave the lieutenant leave to collect the French decoration in Paris. And while he was there, the commander asked, would he be good enough to fly back a new plane for the wing – a Henri Farman.

On Thursday 17 June Reginald received the Legion d'Honneur from none other than General Joffre – known as 'Papa' Joffre, the saviour of France at the Battle of the Marne in 1914. This was followed by a slap-up lunch, after which he went out to Buc airfield to pick up the Farman. Always eager to try new machines, he decided to see what it could do. With an American on board, a journalist eager for a flight with the hero of the moment, Reginald put on a show. He banked and turned through a series of violent manoeuvres, then dived at full power from 1,000 feet (300 m) to zoom over the heads of the admiring crowd.

Abruptly, the perfect day ended. As the Farman climbed out of the dive the wings buckled, the propeller hit the tail boom and the plane disintegrated. Both the pilot and the passenger were catapulted out of the cockpit and plummeted 200 feet (60 m) to earth. Shocked spectators rushed to the scene of the crash and found the journalist dead but Reginald still breathing. Horribly, the Legion d'Honneur had been driven into his chest by the impact. Lieutenant Warneford was rushed to hospital but died of his injuries on the way. The wild hawk was down.

FIGHTING FACTS

RNAS and RFC – Rivals in the Sky

The RFC was set up in 1912 with a military wing to serve with the army and a naval wing to meet the needs of the Royal Navy. From the start, however, the navy wanted control of its own aircraft and soon changed the name of the naval wing to the RNAS. This left the army in sole control of the RFC. Unwisely the RNAS and RFC became rivals, competing for resources and manpower. In 1918 both were merged into the new Royal Air

Force. The RAF became Britain's third armed service, independent of both the army and the navy.

Tolerable Terminology

Like the British Army and the Royal Navy, the German armed services were rivals. The German Navy bought airships from the company owned by Cavalry Officer Graf (Count) von Zeppelin. They were designated L at first or LZ for the larger machines made later in the war. Zeppelins had an aluminium skeleton covered with fabric.

The German Army bought similar airships from a competing firm, Luftschiffbau (*luft*, air; *schiff*, ship) Schutte-Lanz. They were designated SL. The major difference was SLs had a plywood framework instead of a metal one.

These subtleties were lost on the British, however. All enemy airships soon became known as Zeppelins or Zepps, regardless of who made them. (Just like vacuum cleaners today are sometimes called Hoovers, even though Hoover is just one make.)

In this story the term 'Zeppelin' is used loosely to describe any German airship. However, some people can get very worked up about this and, strictly speaking, it's wrong. One writer has attacked 'the welter of ignorance and confusion into which the terminology of lighter-than-air flight has fallen'. But you won't tread on any toes if you know your Zepp from your Schutte-Lanz.

LZ38

Remember the two other pilots who set off on a mission on 7 June? John Wilson and John Mills were ordered to bomb the airship sheds at Evere. They not only found their target in a night raid, they dodged the enemy guns and hit hard. One shed burned down with LZ38 inside – the same airship that had bombed London only the week before!

1916 – Terror from the Skies 2

In 1916, reinforced by a new generation of Zeppelins, the Germans attacked again. The latest ships carried more hydrogen and far more bombs. Peter Strasser, the Leader of Airships, was out to show that his crews could drop enough explosives to damage the British war effort.

The British responded by improving their defences, posting squadrons at key locations down the eastern half of the country. Crucially, the planes were equipped with new ammunition. Throughout 1915 pilots had blazed away with their Lewis guns without any obvious effect. The bullets had simply passed straight through the hydrogen bags, causing nothing but irritating leaks that were quickly patched by the sailmakers aboard the Zepps. It sounds zany, but the Germans had crewmen stitching up holes even while the airships were under attack.

Now the British machine guns fired a deadly mix of Brock or Pomeroy explosive bullets and Buckingham incendiary bullets. (Named after their inventors. Brock also manufactured fireworks.) They made a lethal combination when fired together. The explosive bullets blew holes in the Zeppelin gas bags, allowing the hydrogen to mix with the oxygen in the air. The incendiary bullets then ignited the mixed gases. Result – BOOM! After a long and lucky run against British aircraft, the Germans were in for a shock.

Zeppelin Down

Shortly after 23:00 on 2 September 1916 Lieutenant 'Billy' Leefe Robinson took off from Sutton Farm airfield, near London. A Zeppelin alert had sent the pilots scurrying into the air and he hoped for some action! Climbing his BE2c night-fighter through thick cloud, he levelled off at 3,000 feet (920 m) to patrol between Hornchurch and Joyce Green near Dartford Marshes. After a couple of mind-numbing hours his bleary eyes caught a sharp gleam of light to the east – a Zepp trapped in the beam of a searchlight.

Opening the throttle, Billy set off in hot pursuit. But his excitement soon faded. Long before he was in range, the airship slipped away into the clouds. Ho-hum. Boredom again. What are the chances of spotting two Zepps in one night? Billy wondered. 'None!' he moaned, giving a dismal answer to his own question.

Flying on, in the vain hope that the searchlights might catch another intruder, his wish was suddenly granted.

Le Petit Journal

ADMINISTRATION
61, RUE LAFAYETTE, 61

Les manuscrits ne sont pas rendus

5 CENT. SUPPLÉMENT ILLUSTRÉ 5 CENT.

26ᵐᵉ Année   ——   Numéro 1.279

DIMANCHE 27 JUIN 1915

ABONNEMENTS

LE ZEPPELIN ABATTU

A Zepplin being shot down was a cause of celebration for the Allies

Luck: There it was – SL11. Visible in the flashes of . . .

Bad luck: . . . an intense bombardment of exploding anti-aircraft shells.

Despite the high risk of being shot down by his own side, Billy attacked. As SL11 twisted and turned to escape the ground-fire, he raked the full length of the underbelly with a whole drum of incendiaries.

But nothing happened!

Reloading his Lewis gun, he turned and dived along one side of the airship, again emptying a full drum into the giant.

Still nothing happened!

Could it be that Zepps really were invulnerable?

Attacking a third time, Billy changed his tactics. He put his plane behind and below SL11's massive **elevators** and pumped his last drum into a small area. This time, as the bullets ripped into the airship's frame, a dull pink glow bloomed deep inside the hull. Within seconds flames 100 feet (30 m) long shot out of the doomed raider.

As hot debris fell about him, Billy wrenched his aircraft out of the way. SL11 became a ball of fire visible from 35 miles (56 km) away, before it exploded and hit the ground at Cuffley, a small hamlet in Hertfordshire. This was the show Londoners had waited months to see. They poured out into the streets, singing and clapping as the airship died overhead. One witness was ten-year-old Henry Turtle, living in Islington. He remembered:

THE ZEPPELIN RAIDS : THE VOW OF VENGEANCE
Drawn for 'The Daily Chronicle' by Frank Brangwyn ARA

'DAILY CHRONICLE' READERS ARE
COVERED AGAINST THE RISKS OF
BOMBARDMENT BY ZEPPELIN OR
AEROPLANE

This newspaper illustration mirrors the British public's
horror of Zeppelin attacks on civilian targets

*We opened the front door and there it was: a fantastic
sight like a big silver cigar ... then all of a sudden
flames started to come from the Zeppelin and it broke
in half and was one mass of flames. It was an
incredible sight: people were cheering, dancing and
someone started playing the bagpipes. All the children,
and I was one of them marched up and down cheering
like merry hell. We were told afterwards, at school that
the Zepp was shot down by Lt. Robinson RFC.*

Flu Victim

Billy was awarded the Victoria Cross, the first for an
action over or on British soil. Yet even heroes are
helpless in the face of tiny foes – bugs. In 1918 the worst
flu epidemic in history hit Britain. Over 150,000 people
died and one of them was Billy Robinson.

Air Raid

Night shatters in mid-heaven – the bark of guns,
The roar of planes, the crash of bombs, and all
The unshackled skyey pandemonium stuns
The senses to indifference, when a fall
Of masonry nearby startles awake,
Tingling, wide-eyed, prick eared, with bristling hair,
Each sense within the body, crouched aware
Like some sore-hunted creature in the brake.

Yet side by side we lie in the little room,
Just touching hands, with eyes and ears that strain
Keenly, yet dream-bewildered, through tense gloom,
Listening, in helpless stupor of insane
Drugged nightmare panic fantastically wild,
To the quiet breathing of our little child.

Wilfrid Gibson

GOTHA SUMMER

BATTLE BRIEFING

The Zeppelin raids of 1916 were beaten off with heavy German losses. Together with SL11, a string of other Zeppelins were soon destroyed, including:

- L33 – brought down by ground fire over Bromley, Kent, on 23 September. When it crash-landed in Essex, the crew jumped to safety and set fire to their ship to prevent its capture.
- L32 – snared in searchlights over east London and shot down by Lieutenant Frederick Sowrey during the same raid.
- L31 – shot down over London by Second Lieutenant W. J. Tempest on 2 October. It crashed in flames at Potters Bar, Hertfordshire, and all the crew died. The captain was found embedded in the ground. He was still alive, though soon died of his injuries.

After this gory autumn the myth of the invulnerable airship had been shattered. Even the bravest German crews were daunted and airship raids were scaled back.

As the Zeppelin threat faded, the British dropped their guard. Key pilots from home-defence squadrons were sent to the Western Front, while many of the anti-aircraft guns were fitted to merchant ships for the bitter war against the U-boats (submarines) in the Atlantic.

To release more men for the army – gunners, observers, searchlight operators, etc. could all be retrained as infantrymen – only guns stationed on the coast were allowed to open fire on intruders. Inland anti-aircraft batteries were ordered not to engage the enemy. One explanation for this amazing order was overconfidence. Home Forces Command did not expect a large attack, believing that the German Air Force was simply not up to it. Ironically, just as the British relaxed, the threat from the air was about to take a turn for the worse. By May 1917 the first squadrons of massive Gotha GIV bombers were finally ready and waiting.

THE SLAUGHTER OF THE INNOCENTS

High Stakes

By November 1916 the epic Battle of the Somme had ground to a halt. The British and French had taken a miserable strip of land 30 miles (50 km) long and 7 miles (11 km) deep – at a cost of 600,000 killed, wounded or captured. The terrible waste of young lives made the Somme a bitter symbol of the horror of war. But amidst the carnage there was some gain – German losses were almost as bad. The Kaiser's army was exhausted and needed time to recover and rebuild defences.

To gain time, the German High Command ordered two counter-strokes. The deadliest was at sea. U-boats were ordered to attack and sink enemy ships without mercy. It almost worked. During the spring of 1917 British shipping losses trebled and the war hung in the balance.

To pile on the pressure, and perhaps force the enemy to seek peace, the air force was ordered to attack London, the heart of the Allied war effort. General Ludendorff, a key player in the German High Command, wrote:

The plan was to take from the Allies their faith in victory. The main object was the moral intimidation of the British nation and the crippling of the will to fight.

Crucial targets included government buildings around Downing Street, the Admiralty (HQ of the navy) and the Bank of England. And if nothing else, more air raids would force the British to divert men and resources from the Western Front to home defence.

A New Weapon

To deliver the blow, a crack unit was equipped with the latest long-range planes. Kampfgeschwader 1 (Battle Squadron 1, shortened to Kagohl 1 and, just to complicate matters, renamed Kagohl 3) had aerodromes at St Denis Westrem and Melle-Gontrode, near Ghent, in Belgium. Led by an inspiring commander, Hauptmann Ernest Brandenburg, the pilots had been eager to have a crack at London since 1914. And now they were being given the tool to do it.

The GIV biplane bomber was nicknamed the Gotha after the company who made it, Gothaer Waggonfabrik AG. It was an awesome size. The fuselage was over 40 feet long (12 m) and the wingspan almost 78 feet (24 m). Powered by two 260-hp (horsepower) Mercedes engines, it had a maximum speed of 87 mph (140 kph) at 12,000 feet (3,700 m). The crew of three sat in a roomy cockpit, with a walkway between the seats. At the front was the commander. And just to make sure he had no time for dozing, he was also observer/navigator/bomb aimer and front gunner. Next came the pilot and behind him sat the rear gunner.

The GIV was armed with three 7.92-mm Parabellum machine guns, one at the front and two at the back. This clever design gave the rear gunner a choice of weapons and proved a nasty shock to British pilots attacking from behind. One gun was mounted to fire above the fuselage, but the second swivelled to shoot through a

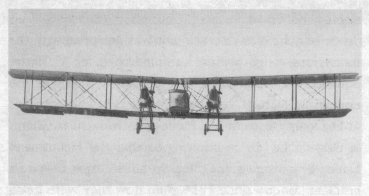

The Gotha G5

tunnel, spraying the area under the tail. To make sure they didn't freeze up at high altitudes, the guns were electrically heated, the power coming from a dynamo driven by the right-hand engine. The ammo drums held 200 rounds.

The bomb load depended upon the height of a raid. During the day the Gotha attacked from as high as 18,000 feet (5,540 m) and could only carry 700 lb (320 kg) of bombs. At night, when it flew lower, at 10,000 feet (3,080 m), the load was increased to 1,000 lb (455 kg). In early raids, the heaviest German bombs weighed 110 lb (50 kg) but, luckily for London, poor fuses meant that a third of those dropped were duds, while another 10 per cent exploded in the air.

First Raids
By mid-May 1917 the pilots of Kagohl 3 were fully

trained and itching for action, but poor weather held up the first attack. It was not until 25 May that days of thunderstorms passed and the sun shone. At 15:30 the bombers lumbered into the air and set course for England.

The main target was London, but as the Gothas came in over Essex, Brandenburg saw that the capital was hidden by dense cloud. Disappointed, but determined to hit the enemy hard, he fired signal flares to turn his force south into Kent. At 16:30 half the force attacked Shorncliffe Camp, a huge undefended army base full of Canadian troops. Twenty-seven bombs were dropped, one falling on a company of soldiers preparing for an evening route march. There was carnage among the neat, unsuspecting ranks – 17 were killed and 93 wounded.

A few minutes later the raiders hit Folkestone. It was Friday evening, pay night, just before the Whitsun holiday, and the streets were packed with shoppers. One bomb fell in the queue outside Stokes Grocer's, killing or seriously injuring 60 people, many of them children.

The Gothas had first been sighted at 16:45, yet for almost 2 hours they roamed through English airspace at will. Defences had been poorly coordinated and most anti-aircraft guns had obeyed the order not to open fire. Few gunners had realized this was a serious attack, not just a pin-prick raid by a couple of aircraft. Navy fighters did manage to shoot down two Gothas, but the rest of Kagohl 3 escaped almost without a scratch. Exactly as the Germans planned, the British public were shocked – and a little scared.

Target London

A second Gotha raid set out for London on 5 June, but this time British defences were much sharper. Faced with heavy anti-aircraft fire, the bombers turned instead towards their back-up target, the dockyard town of Sheerness. In a 5-minute attack, 13 people died and another 34 were injured. Gotha 660 was shot down into the sea.

A week later, on Wednesday 13 June, Kagohl 3 tried again. This time the forecasters promised perfect flying weather until late afternoon, when thunderstorms would break. To make best use of the day, the squadron took off from Belgium at 09:00. They would reach London at midday, when the British capital was at its busiest, and be back home before the weather broke.

By 10:30 20 raiders were nearing the North Foreland, near Shoeburyness, and since this was the third assault they expected a hard time from the enemy defences. However, to create as much confusion as possible, Brandenburg had prepared a double-decoy. He raised his flare-gun into the slipstream and fired – a prearranged signal for a lone machine to peel off and bomb Margate. At 10:45 the pilot began his attack run and dropped four bombs, causing little damage. But this didn't matter. He had raised a hornet's nest and set off for home, chased by nine vital fighters from Manston aerodrome. None was back in time to intercept the main force.

At 10:50, as the Gothas approached the Essex coast near the mouth of the River Crouch, two more planes left the formation and attacked Shoeburyness. This time the ruse failed. The bombers turned for home without any British fighters in pursuit.

By about 11:40 the Germans were wheeling over central London. The weather was perfect for the raiders – patchy cloud at about 5,000 feet (1,540 m), making it hard for anti-aircraft gunners to get a clear shot. Yet, viewed from 14,000 feet (4,300 m), the sparkling glass

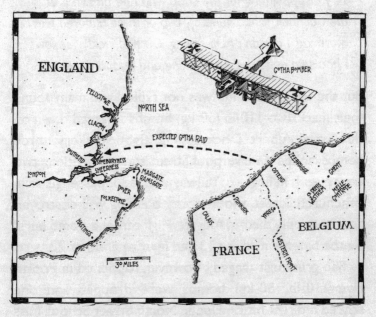

The route the Gotha bombers took

roof of Liverpool Street station shone like a navigation beacon in the hazy sunshine.

On the streets below, Londoners heard the drone of engines but were still unaware of the danger. One RFC pilot, Lieutenant Charles Chabot was among the crowds.

> I was up in town on a day's leave ... wandering as an ordinary civilian down Cheapside ... when the raid started. Raids hadn't become a very serious thing and everybody crowded into the street to watch. They didn't take cover or dodge. A bomb went off right over the Guildhall and it seemed to me, having had quite a bit of experience of dropping bombs myself, that it was very disappointing for the chap who had thrown it at the Guildhall. It had gone off two or three hundred feet overhead. I couldn't help saying, 'Oh bad luck!' ... I saw I had said quite the wrong thing and had to make off.

But the Guildhall bomb was not typical and many found their mark. Two 110-lb (50-kg) bombs smashed down on the Royal Albert Dock, killing eight workers; three bombs landed on Liverpool Street station, wrecking two trains and killing 16 railwaymen and passengers; in Fenchurch Street a four-storey building was destroyed and 20 people died; in Aldgate High Street a bomb burst on the pavement, killing 13 and injuring another 22.

The grimmest tragedy, however, happened in Poplar. Five 110-lb (50-kg) bombs were dropped and one scored a direct hit on Upper North Street School. Miss

I. A. Major remembered the raiders passing overhead:

Our teachers had been warned of an approaching air raid and were endeavouring to keep us all calm by getting us to sing together. Soon, however, the noise of the anti-aircraft guns and the detonation of the enemy bombs sounded above even our shrill voices.

The bomb crashed through three floors and exploded in the infants' class on the ground floor, where 64 children had gathered. Esther Levy was in a nearby classroom. She recalled:

There was a tremendous bang and of course everybody was panic-stricken. A big fat girl called Kitty Chalmers fell on top of me ... but I picked myself up. The teachers were marvellous. They were saying 'Don't panic' and 'File down quietly' ... I distinctly remember one of the teachers carrying a girl – I think her name was Pittard – whose leg was severed. What really frightened me was seeing all those little children being carried out. They were all black and their hair ginger from TNT [explosive].

Rescue workers were shocked by the carnage they found in the school. Eighteen children were killed outright and another 30 had terrible injuries. Mrs Myers, then an older pupil, desperately looked for her younger sister in the wreckage of the school:

I forced my way along the corridor filled with men and

*women frantically searching for their children. All were
screaming and shouting. I could not find her anywhere
and it was two hours later when my father found her
dead in the mortuary.*

Telegraphic Address:
"Schools, Estrand, London."
Telephone No.
10,000 Gerrard.

London County Council.

AT THE HEAD
OF YOUR REPLY
PLEASE WRITE

Education Offices,

Victoria Embankment, W.C. 2.

20th June, 1917.

Dear Mr. Brewis,

As Chairman of the Education Committee for London I
feel that I must write you a few lines of heartfelt sympathy.
The injury to your little girl Catherine through the sudden and
terrifying disaster of last Wednesday, 13th June, must have been
a very severe blow to you. It may, however, be some comfort to
you to know that so many people are thinking of you in your
trouble. In the days to come your little girl will be remembered
as one who suffered for her country just as much as if she had
been a soldier wounded while fighting at the front. My sincere
sympathy is with you.

The Minister for Education, Mr. Herbert Fisher, asks
me to convey to you his warmest sympathy.

Yours very sincerely,

[signature]

Chairman of the Education Committee.

Mr. J. G. Brewis,
54, Gough Street,
E.14.

A letter of sympathy to the parents of a girl wounded in the bombing of Upper North
Street School, east London, in June 1917

A Disgrace to the Empire

By midday the Gothas had finished their attack and were approaching Southend, on their way back to Belgium. They had run the gauntlet of anti-aircraft guns but none had been hit. More humiliating for the British, over 90 RFC fighters took off to catch Kagohl 3, yet only 12 came close enough to open fire. And even these were soon outdistanced by the German planes, travelling higher and faster since they had dropped their bombs.

One of those taking part in the hunt was Captain James McCudden, by now a proud pilot. He wrote a vivid account of the maddening action:

I took off in an easterly direction. At 5,000 feet I climbed into woolly clouds and not until I reached 10,000 feet did I see the ground again through small gaps between the clouds. It was an ideal day for a bombing formation to get to their objective unobserved.

I caught up with them at the expense of some height and by the time I got under the rear machine I was 1,000 feet below. I now found that there were over 20 machines, all with two 'pusher' engines. To my dismay I could not lessen the range to any appreciable extent. By the time I had got to 500 feet under the rear machine we were 20 miles off the Essex coast, and visions of a very long swim entered my mind, so I decided to fire all my ammunition and then depart.

I fired my first drum, of which the Hun did not take

the slightest notice. I now perceived another Sopwith Pup just behind this rear Hun at quite close range, but after a while he turned away as though he was experiencing some trouble with his gun.

How insolent these damn Boches did look, absolutely lording the sky above England! I replaced my first drum with another and had another try, after which the Hun swerved ever so slightly, and that welcome sound of machine-guns smote my ears and I caught the smell of the Hun's incendiary bullets as they passed me. I now put on my third and last single Lewis drum [each drum held 47 shots] and fired again. To my intense chagrin, the last Hun did not take the slightest notice.

The Gothas' luck held all the way home. RNAS fighters from Dunkirk had been **scrambled** but failed to spot the returning bombers. At about 14:00 Kagohl 3 landed at its bases without mishap. Half an hour later the weather broke in a furious storm, with heavy rain and hailstones as large as pigeon's eggs. If the British defences had simply managed to slow down the Gothas, then they would have been caught in that maelstrom and several most likely wrecked.

Brandenburg was delighted with the results of the raid. His airmen had certainly wrenched the tail of the British lion, just as Ludendorff had ordered. And they had created a wave of terror – 162 people were killed and 432 injured, the most punishing raid of the whole war. In London there was outrage that 16 enemy bombers could roam at will over the capital of the greatest empire on earth without being challenged. 'What has gone wrong?' the newspapers demanded. 'And what is being done about it?'

FIGHTING FACTS

The Carrier Pigeon Squadron

Bombing London using aeroplanes had always been part of German plans to win the war. In 1914 Major General Siegert, a former balloon pilot, took charge of just such a force. It was codenamed the Carrier Pigeon Squadron to fool enemy spies. He faced two problems:

One: The 36 B-type bombers he was given were underpowered and could carry only small loads.

Two: The B-types had a short range and needed an airfield near Calais if they were to reach London. Siegert was robbed of this when the German advance was stopped in October 1914. Bases were set up in Belgium but they were too far away. The Carrier Pigeon Squadron had to make do with attacks on Allied aerodromes on the Western Front.

The plan to bomb London was filed away but not forgotten. The German Air Force issued specifications for a Grosskampfflugzeug (a large bomber aircraft) – the

G-type – and several companies, including Gothaer Waggonfabrik AG, set to work on designs.

The Blue Max

When Kagohl 3 landed back in Belgium on 13 June 1917, it was to a hero's welcome. Kaiser Wilhelm II was delighted with the results of the attack and ordered that Hauptmann Brandenburg be presented to him at Supreme Headquarters at Kreuznach in southern Germany.

The following day Brandenburg flew the 200 miles (320 km) to Kreuznach in a two-seater Albatros, piloted by Oberleutnant von Trotha. The meeting went well. The Kaiser listened closely to Brandenburg's tale of the raid and presented him with the Blue Max – the highly prized medal held by top German aces like Max Immelman and Manfred von Richthofen, known as the Red Baron.

Early on the morning of Tuesday 19 June, with von Trotha at the controls again, Brandenburg set out to return to Kagohl 3. Shortly after take-off the engine stalled and the Albatros spun to earth. The pilot died instantly and Brandenburg was severely injured – his legs crushed. Sheer bad luck had achieved more than the combined efforts of all the British defences. Kagohl 3 had lost a great leader – and never performed as well again as a fighting unit.

Losing the Propaganda War

At first the Germans were thrilled with the results of

the 13 June raid. An apology was sent for the deaths of the civilians, especially the children. The message nevertheless went on to blame the British government for these unnecessary losses, saying residents should have been moved away from military targets such as Sheerness and London.

In reality the German High Command knew that attacks on England would cause civilian casualties – and considered this no bad thing. It was believed this would add to the terror of the raids and shake British morale. The only German newspaper to condemn the attacks on London was closed down.

But the plan backfired. The British people were shocked and horrified by the deaths of the Poplar children. It was the worst outrage since the sinking of the passenger liner *Lusitania* by a U-boat in 1915. The tragedy seemed to prove that the war against such a barbaric enemy *had* to be won. Far from weakening the fighting spirit of the British, the Germans found they had rekindled it.

Duff Defence

The defence of London had been a shambles. The list of clangers was a long one:

- Too many British home-defence fighters were old-fashioned machines like the BE2c, the FE2b and the BE12. They were fine for tackling Zeppelins at night but not much else. Even the best of them, the BE12, could only just claw its way to 13,000 feet (4,000 m) –

not high enough to catch the Gothas. Only a handful of fighters – Sopwith 1^{1}/$_{2}$ Strutters, Camels or Pups – had the speed and ceiling to bring the bombers down. If they could intercept in time . . .

- Attack warnings took too long to reach fighter airfields. By the time the fighters had scrambled and climbed to 14,000 feet (4,300 m), the Gothas were already on their way home.

- Home-defence pilots were used to operating on their own at night. They had little experience of working together against armed formations of enemy planes. During the raid on 13 June, 94 fighters took off to intercept the Gothas, but only 12 came close enough to open fire. None of the pilots coordinated an attack with another aircraft.

- British machine guns jammed too often because of faulty ammunition. Flight Lieutenant Fox, flying a Sopwith Pup, attacked a Gotha at 14,000 feet over Southend. His tracer bullets were licking the enemy fuselage when his Lewis gun seized up. Furious, all he could do was drop out of the fight.

- Anti-aircraft fire had been piecemeal and inaccurate. No enemy planes were hit, but at least one British fighter had been badly damaged. Worse, two people were killed and 18 others injured by falling shell splinters. This had happened because their cases were not blown into small enough pieces when shells exploded.

- Air-raid warnings were given only to people working in likely targets, to avoid disrupting war work and causing panic. Some civilian casualties occurred among people who had poured out on to the streets to look at the Gothas flying overhead.

Getting It Right

The Germans had been wrong about the Gotha raids sapping Britain's will to fight. But they were correct about forcing the British to use up valuable resources to defend their capital city. Faced with a huge public outcry, the government responded with a number of urgent improvements to home defence.

- **Improvement:** The London Air Defence Area was set up to pull together control of air-raid warnings, fighters, guns and searchlights. Aeroplanes fitted with radios patrolled the skies to track bomber formations and report their speed and direction. An operations room plotted incoming raiders on a large squared map and direct telephone lines were installed to warn airfields and gun sites.
- **Improvement:** Three new squadrons of top-class fighters were formed – but at a cost! The men and machines were urgently needed in France, where losses were mounting calamitously. By August 1917 a further 150 new fighters had been delivered to other units.

- **Improvement:** The Green Line – a ring of anti-aircraft guns round the east of London – was set up to fire a mass of exploding shells at incoming bombers. It was hoped that this barrage would break up the tight formations of Gothas and make them easier prey for fighters.

- **Improvement:** Air-raid warnings were given over a large area using rockets and policemen blowing whistles. Sirens, unlike those used in World War II, were not loud enough to be heard over the roar of London traffic.

An Irish Airman Foresees His Death

I know that I shall meet my fate
Somewhere among the clouds above;
Those that I fight I do not hate,
Those that I guard I do not love;
My country is Kiltartan Cross,
My countrymen Kiltartan's poor,
No likely end could bring them loss
Or leave them happier than before.
Nor law, nor duty bade me fight,
Nor public men, nor cheering crowds,
A lonely impulse of delight
Drove to this tumult in the clouds;
I balanced all, brought all to mind,
The years to come seemed waste of breath,
A waste of breath the years behind
In balance with this life, this death.

W. B. Yeats

ACE OF
ACES

BATTLE BRIEFING

The Somme

On 1 July 1916 the British Army began the great attack on the Somme. A massive bombardment had swept enemy lines for days, firing over 1,700,000 shells. The troops were told that this would destroy the German defences and that the advance would be a walkover. It wasn't. On the first day of the 'big push' 57,000 men were killed or injured – and the battle rolled grimly on until 18 November.

During the long Somme campaign the RFC did everything that was asked of it . . . and more. The 'Fokker scourge' was beaten and for most of the battle British planes controlled the skies. With the arrival of faster fighters, like the DH2 and the Sopwith Pup, the RFC developed new tactics. Orders stated that scouts should stay close to the reconnaissance machines they were protecting, but some plucky pilots realized that it was more efficient to go 'looking for the enemy rather than waiting for him to find you'.

In their battered trenches the infantry had a worm's-eye view of the fighting in the air. Captain Arthur Gibbs of the Welsh Guards wrote:

> Our aeroplanes are magnificent all day and every day. They fly low over our line, and the Boche line, and see exactly where we are and what is going on ... Any Boche plane that puts its nose out of port is jolly soon chased back again.

Even the German High Command admitted in a frank report:

> The first weeks of the Somme battle were marked by the complete inferiority of our own air forces. The enemy's aeroplanes enjoyed complete freedom in carrying out distant reconnaissances. With the aid of aeroplane observation, the hostile artillery neutralized our guns and was able to range with extreme accuracy on the trenches occupied by our infantry.

The Albatros

When the German reply came, it was deadly. Reinforcements flooded into the Somme sector but, crucially, their scouts were organized into new hunting or fighting squadrons called Jastas. Pilots were no longer lone wolves but operated in killer teams of 14 machines.

Worse still for the British, in September 1916 a new German plane reached the battlefront – the Albatros DI. This was a brilliant aircraft, fitted with two synchronized machine guns firing through the propeller arc. The 160-hp Mercedes engines gave a top speed of 105 mph (168 kph) and a ceiling of 14,000 feet (4,300 m). Soon, the balance of power in the air flipped back to Germany and the RFC suffered heavily. During the Somme campaign 359 German planes were destroyed and 43 pilots killed at a cost of 800 British machines and 252 RFC pilots.

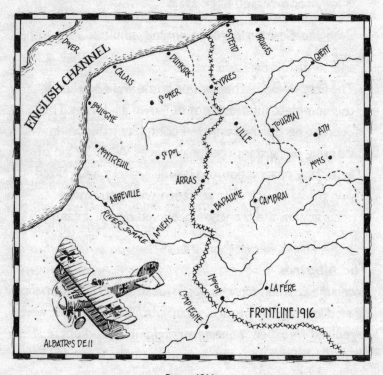

France, 1916

Arras

In April 1917 the British Fifth Army began a new offensive near Arras and once again the RFC was ordered to sweep the skies of German aircraft. But this time the plan went dreadfully wrong. Now 37 Jastas patrolled enemy lines. The pilots had been hand-picked for their skills in single-seater fighters and most flew the Albatros, including the latest – DIII.

As the British reconnaissance machines and their guarding scouts flew over German lines, the Jastas climbed into the sun and waited. The up-and-coming ace, Manfred von Richthofen wrote:

It is better if the customers come to the shop.
Certainly they are brave, but it is a bravery with a touch of foolishness about it.

The air battle over Arras would be remembered as 'Bloody April' by the RFC. One hundred and fifty planes were shot down, 28 on Easter Sunday alone. The flying life of a fighter pilot fell to $17^{1}/2$ hours. And in the months that followed the slaughter continued. Into this butchery flew one man who soon became a match for the best German aces – Edward 'Mick' Mannock. However the first weeks of his career were anything but promising.

MICK MANNOCK – THE MAKING OF AN ACE

Too Cocky by Half

Have you ever been in the wrong place at the wrong time? Or been in trouble because you've got a big mouth? Then you may feel a little sympathy for Mick Mannock. On 6 April 1917 he suffered from both problems when he joined 40 Squadron at their base at Aire in France. Unfortunately, first impressions do count and the poor showing Mick made that day dogged him for weeks.

At best, 6 April was a bad day to join the squadron. They had just been in action and been badly mauled by the Germans, losing a popular pilot, Lieutenant Pell. The mood in the mess was dour and the last thing they needed was an insensitive jerk. Enter the new boy, ready to insert foot in mouth. Mick didn't know what had happened, but then again he didn't give anyone a chance to tell him.

He walked in and plonked himself in Pell's usual chair. Whoops! It was good manners to leave a dead pilot's seat vacant for a few days, a small memorial to an absent friend. Then he began to sound off: 'Let me tell you what I think of the war ... blah, blah. My opinion on aerial combat is ... blah, blah. You've just converted from FE8s to Nieuport 17s? Well, I've been training on ... blah, blah. What's your name? And how many Germans have you shot down?'

232

Mick Mannock during training with the RFC, 1916

Lieutenant Blaxland remembered:

He seemed too cocky for his experience, which was nil. New men usually took their time and listened to the more experienced hands. Most men in his position, by that I mean a man from his background and with his lack of fighting experience, would have shut up and

*earned their place in the mess. He seemed a boorish
know-all and we all felt the quicker he got amongst the
Huns the better.*

An Unusual Recruit

His new unit wouldn't have guessed, but Mannock's
brash manner was a mask to hide his nerves. He was 28
when he qualified as a pilot, much older than most new
recruits, who were little more than boys. His
background was different too – he was definitely not a
gentleman. He was probably born in Cork in Ireland (see
pages 112–13), hence the nickname 'Mick'. He had had a
working-class upbringing and had never set foot in a
posh public school.

Mick had seen the hard side of life. His father was a
soldier who had abandoned his mother, leaving her to
bring up the family in poverty. Mick had left school at 14
to start work in a grocer's shop before he eventually
became a telephone engineer. When war broke out in
Europe he was working to install a telephone system in
Turkey. It was an unfortunate place to be.

In 1915 Turkey joined the war on the German side
and Mick was interned. He almost starved to death in
the **internment camp** and carried a virulent hatred
of Germans from then on. It was German officers who
had asked the Turks to lock up British civilians and they
had done nothing to ease the dreadful conditions in
the camps.

After Mick had been repatriated (sent home in a deal brokered by the Americans) he joined the army and then requested a transfer to the RFC. He was bright, determined and quickly became a top student. One instructor wrote:

> He made his first solo flight in a Henri Farman with only a few hours' instruction. He seemed to master the rudiments of flying in his first hour in the air and from then on threw the machine about as he pleased.

Perhaps Mick could be forgiven, then, for thinking that he had qualities to offer 40 Squadron . . . if his fellow pilots would give him a second chance. But the coming days didn't improve matters.

A Windy Type

On his first patrols Mick seemed edgy. He'd make silly mistakes, wrongly setting his engine and dropping out of formation. His plane was the last to make a move and he seemed to lack energy and drive. The rumour went round that Mannock was a 'windy type' – a coward. And after his first combat experience, even Mick began to wonder if he had the nerve to be a fighter pilot.

On 13 April six planes from 40 Squadron crossed German lines, escorting RE8 reconnaissance planes. Soon they ran into heavy flak and the aircraft were bounced around the sky. As **Archie** exploded nearby Mick felt an awful dryness in his mouth and throat, and his stomach heaved. It was the sensation of cold unrelenting fear – and it didn't get any better during his next flights.

Fortune wasn't on Mick's side either. He was desperate to make his first kill and prove himself, but there always seemed to be a problem. On 1 May he was on patrol with his new flight commander, Captain Keen. The mission was risky, to photograph Douai aerodrome, the home of Manfred von Richthofen's Jasta. Mick wrote a vivid report in his diary:

> We were attacked from above over Douai. I tried my gun going over German lines, only to find that it was jammed, so I went over with a revolver only. A Hun in a beautiful yellow and green 'bus' attacked me from behind. I could hear his machine-gun cracking away. I wheeled round on him and howled like a dervish (although of course he couldn't hear me) whereat he made off towards old Parry and attacked him, with me following for the moral effect! Another one (a brown speckled one) attacked a Sopwith, and Keen blew the pilot to pieces & the Hun went spinning down from 12,000 feet to earth. Unfortunately the Sopwith had been hit and went down too, and there was I a passenger, absolutely helpless, an easy prey to any of them ... What is the good of it all?

Six days later Mick learned another lesson about the wastage of war. A flight (six aircraft) from 40 Squadron went on a balloon-busting operation. Led by Captain

Nixon, they flew barely 20 feet (6 m) above the ground for a hair-raising 5 miles (8 km) behind enemy lines. It was a lively trip. Again and again they breasted waves of ground fire until, balloons in sight, Nixon pointed each man to his target.

Nieuport 17 planes firing at balloons

Mick pulled down his goggles and arrowed his Nieuport towards the fat brown slug floating on the end of the cable. Pulling the trigger, he fired a burst of tracer and explosive bullets from point-blank range – and watched with delight as the balloon crumpled in flames. Mission accomplished, he put his head down below the cockpit **coaming** and headed for home.

When he landed Mick was euphoric.

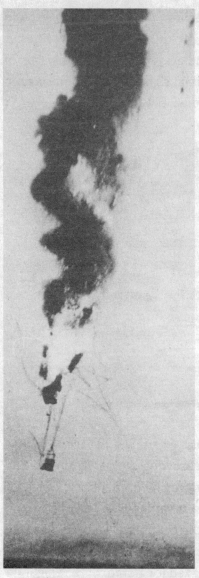

Two German balloons shot down in France

I was the only one to return properly to the aerodrome, and made a perfect landing. We all got our objectives. My fuselage had bullet holes in it, one very near my head, and the wings were more or less riddled.

Then he heard the bad news. Just as the attack had gone in, Captain Nixon had scanned the horizon and spotted five Albatros DIIIs high above and ready to pounce. Knowing his unit was at a terrible disadvantage, he peeled off and climbed to meet the enemy. In a brief, wheeling dogfight Nixon was hopelessly outnumbered and shot down. His killer was Lothar von Richthofen, the brother of the Red Baron.

Practice Makes Perfect

While Mick was a competent, even skilful pilot, he wasn't a 'natural' like the Canadian Billy Bishop or England's favourite ace, Albert Ball. He had to work hard to improve and to overcome his own doubts. He carefully studied single-seater tactics and, crucially, developed his marksmanship.

Mick's spare hours were spent with his Nieuport pulled close to the butts while a bored mechanic yelled out the results of firing tests. Sitting on the edge of the cockpit, he would fine-tune the Lewis gun on the upper wing and align the sight on the front cowling. Again and again Mick would fire short bursts until he had the bullet pattern he wanted – a close group at a range of only 90–120 feet (28–37 m). After this came endless practice with the ground target, pulling out of screaming dives, guns blazing, only a few feet from impact. Now all he needed was that elusive change of luck. It finally came in June.

On 7 June Mick was escorting a formation of FE2b bombers to raid the town of Lille. Within seconds of their arrival over the target the bombers were jumped by a flight of Albatros scouts and Mick's flight of Nieuports went to the rescue. Picking out a German who was closing in on an FE, Mick attacked. That night he wrote in his diary:

My man gave me an easy mark. I was only 10 yards away from him – on top so I couldn't miss! A beautiful coloured insect he was – red, blue, green & yellow. I let him have 60 rounds at that range so there wasn't much left of him. I saw him going spinning and slipping down from 14,000.

Although Mick had hated Germans since his imprisonment, he was still shaken by the death of his enemies, as his next confirmed victory showed. After a period of leave in England he was soon back in action and eager to add to his score. On 12 July he set out to look for trouble over German lines and found it south-east of Lens.

He caught sight of two DFW two-seaters in the distance, turned away from them and climbed to 11,000 feet (3,400 m). Manoeuvring above and behind his victims, he dived on the one at the back and let loose a long burst of 90 rounds. The big machine flipped into a dive – out of control. Watching from 7,000 feet (2,150 m) Mick saw the DFW pile into the ground upside down behind British lines at Avion. When he landed he set out immediately for the crash site. It was to leave him with a lasting and troubled memory.

The DFW lay in a crumpled heap. The observer had been wounded and taken to hospital but the pilot had been killed. Mick was nauseated by the sight of the dead pilot and also a dead dog:

Mick Mannock firing at German planes

I gathered a few souvenirs, though the infantry had the first pick. The machine was completely smashed ... I felt exactly like a murderer. The journey to the trenches was rather nauseating ... This sort of thing ... combined to upset me for days.

Yet there was a hard and practical side to this grim visit as well. Mick was still unsure about his shooting. Was he hitting the target? How well were his bullets grouping? The body of the pilot gave him the answer. In a conversation with a friend he explained: 'It sickened me but I had to see where my shots had gone. Do you know there were three neat little bullet holes right here,'

241

pointing to the side of his head. 'I had to find out and this one down on our side was my only chance.'

Flight Command

As his victories mounted Mick came to be accepted and liked by most of the pilots of 40 Squadron. In August 1917 he was promoted to commander of A Flight and began the work that was to make him an outstanding leader. More than most RFC pilots he realized that the days of the lone-wolf ace were coming to an end. Teamwork was the key to success.

In combat Mick became less dashing and reckless, thinking through new tactics with endless planning meetings. He shared his ideas and built the confidence of his men. In the air A Flight practised formation attacks, stalking the enemy to look for a favourable position before pouncing. Crucially, new pilots were nursed until they had the skills to look after themselves. In five months Mick had grown from big-mouthed rookie to accomplished commander of the best flight in the squadron. It was only the start of an amazing career.

FIGHTING FACTS

Aces High

Pilots who shot down large numbers of enemy machines

became known as 'aces'. In a war where most men died anonymously, mown down by machine guns or searing artillery barrages, aces captured the public imagination. They seemed almost like knights of old, riding into a glamorous tournament in the air.

In Europe aces were treated like pop stars and became instant celebrities. Their pictures and autographs were collectors' items and they were mobbed by admiring crowds when they made public appearances.

Wartime Star – Germany

Max Immelman was Germany's first great ace. He was invited to dinner with the King of Bavaria. His Fokker was put on display in Berlin and he was inundated with fan mail.

Wartime Star – France

Georges Guynemer was awarded 15,000 francs by the Michelin tyre company, but in a typically grand gesture gave it away to a charity for the wounded.

Not at All British

In a stuffy British way, the RFC frowned on the idea of aces. General Haig, Commander in Chief of the British Army in France, wrote in 1917:

I feel sure that officers of the RFC are proud of being anonymous like their comrades in other branches of the British Army.

Even Hugh Trenchard, Commander of the RFC, thought aces were overrated. He commented, 'A bomber raid on an enemy airfield can destroy more planes than all the aces in a week.' But he could see that aces had propaganda value and that their heroism could inspire other pilots.

The Top Ten British Empire Aces

An ace added to his score by shooting down or forcing down an enemy plane or airship. It still counted as a victory whether the enemy pilot was killed or not.

Name	Victories	Nationality
1. William Bishop	72	Canadian
2. Edward 'Mick' Mannock	61	British
3. Raymond Collishaw	60	Canadian
4. James McCudden	57	British
5. Anthony Beauchamp-Proctor	54	South African
6. Donald MacLaren	54	Canadian
7. William Barker	50	Canadian
8. Robert Little	47	Australian
9. George McElroy	47	Irish
10. Albert Ball	44	British

Mannock – Whose Ace, Ireland's or England's?

Mick's origins are a point of controversy. Although Edward Mannock was nicknamed 'Mick', his Irish connections may not have been that strong. His father,

Corporal Edward Mannock, was Scottish and his mother, Julia, was English, though possibly from Irish descent. Different accounts have him born in Brighton, Aldershot and Ballincollig, County Cork.

The Irish didn't push too strongly to claim Mick as their own because he was a Unionist. He believed Ireland should remain part of Britain at a time when the Irish struggle for independence was about to gain momentum. It was typical 'Mick', never afraid of an argument or an outspoken opinion.

Mick's Nightmare

Mick's problem with nerves never left him. Time and again he had to fight back his fears to take to the air. His worst nightmare was fire. On 4 September 1917 he shot down four aircraft. The last was a DFW two-seater that burst into flames and turned into a fireball. This kill stayed with him and hounded the dark parts of his mind. By 1918 he was suffering from exhaustion, caused by constant combat, and he began to take a sickening pleasure in seeing his victims on fire.

Mick was determined never to die that way. 'I'll put a bullet through my head if the machine catches fire . . . they'll never burn me,' he declared. But there is an old saying: If you want to make God laugh tell him your plans.

On 26 July 1918 Mick was shot down by ground fire. He had disobeyed one of his own rules – never follow the victim down. Horribly, his plane crashed in flames.

Lieutenant Donald Inglis was flying alongside Mick when he was shot down. He reported:

> Mick fired at a two-seater. He must have got the observer, as the Hun stopped shooting. I fired and hit the Hun's petrol tank. Falling in behind Mick again, we did a couple of turns over the burning wreck and then made for home. We were fairly low, then I saw a flame come out of the side of his machine; it grew bigger and bigger. He went into a slow right-hand turn, about twice, and hit the ground in a burst of flame.

Richthofen's Flying Circus

In the summer of 1917 the Germans refined their tactics again, grouping Jastas together into Jagdgeschwader (JG for short) or mobile fighter wings. Manfred von Richthofen was put in charge of JG No. 1 on 26 July. The unit was housed in tents and portable sheds that could

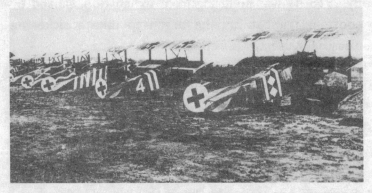

Richthofen's Flying Circus

be transported by train or lorry to any part of the battlefront where there was a crisis.

Pilots painted their machines in striking colours. One British pilot recalled fighting 'machines with green wings and yellow noses, silver wings and gold noses, red bodies with green wings, light blue bodies and red wings'. British airmen soon nicknamed JG 1 'The Flying Circus' because it moved around under canvas like a travelling circus and because of its garishly coloured aircraft. By 1918 there were four circuses flying over the Western Front, savaging the RFC whenever they took to the air.

The Red Baron

Of all the aces of World War I, Baron Manfred von Richthofen, the Red Baron, was the most famous. He learned his flying skills on the Eastern Front against Russia and joined the fighting on the Western Front in 1916. He made his first kill on 17 September and his most notable two months later when he shot down the British ace Lanoe Hawker. Richthofen wrote:

When he [Lanoe] had come down to about 300 feet he tried to escape by flying in a zigzag course. I followed him from an altitude of from 250 feet to 150, firing all the time. The Englishman could not help falling . . . shot through the head.

Cool and steady in combat, Richtofen avoided

unnecessary risks and took his score up to 80, making his last two kills on 20 April 1918. The next day, in an unusually reckless attack, he chased his prey low over Allied lines on the Somme and was shot down by a combination of ground fire and the efforts of Canadian pilot Captain Roy Brown. Although badly wounded, Richthofen managed to land his Fokker triplane on a roadside, but died of his wounds. The Red Baron was buried by the RAF with full military honours.

Golden Rules for Staying Alive

Some aces stayed tight-lipped about their trade secrets. Their main aim was to build up their own scores. Others, like Mick Mannock, made a point of sharing their top fighting tips with young pilots. He realized that the only way to spike the circuses was through teamwork. By 1918 instructions to a rookie pilot would have gone something like this:

- Fly high and keep the sun behind you. **Beware the Hun in the sun!** If you start an attack, always finish it. Remember Mannock's tip: 'Gentlemen, always above; seldom on the same level; never underneath.'
- Try to attack from behind and stay there till you shoot the enemy down.
- If a Hun dives on you, don't try to evade him, turn and meet him head on.
- Never relax your concentration. Always know what is going on around you. Constantly scan the horizon,

looking for danger. What are those specks in the distance?

- Learn to use the clouds. If you fly just within the cloud fringe you will be invisible from below but still able to see what is going on underneath you.
- Stay in formation – killing is teamwork.
- If you are caught napping, get the hell out of it. He who fights and runs away, lives to fight another day.
- Think of your aircraft as a flying rifle and hold it steady. Yes, an ace like McCudden can hit a German at 1,200 feet (370 m), but most pilots can't – get in close.
- Spend your spare time at the shooting butts. Check the firing pattern of your guns and align them yourself for the range you want. Ira Jones likes to open fire at 225 feet (70 m), the Frenchman Fonck from 120–180 feet (37–56 m).
- Don't waste bullets – fire your machine guns in short bursts. The German Max Immelman claimed a kill with every 12 to 25 bullets. Load your own guns to avoid jams from defective bullets or belts.
- Know your aircraft and modify it to scrape out every bit of performance you can. McCudden **machined the cylinder heads** of his SE5a and pushed the ceiling 3,000 feet (923 m) over the official figure.

We Haven't Got a Hope in the Morning

To the tune of 'John Peel'

When you soar into the air in a Sopwith Scout,
And you're scrapping with a Hun and your guns cut out,
Well, you stuff down your nose till your plugs* fall out,
'Cos you haven't got a hope in the morning.

For a batman† woke me from my bed,
I'd had a thick night and a very sore head,
And I said to myself, to myself I said,
'Oh we haven't got a hope in the morning.'

So I went to the sheds and examined my gun,
then my engine I tried to run;
And the revs that it gave were a thousand and one;
'Cos you haven't got a hope in the morning.

For a batman woke me from my bed, etc.

We were escorting Twenty-two,
Hadn't a notion what to do,
So we shot down a Hun and an FE△ too,
'Cos you haven't got a hope in the morning.

* plugs: spark plugs in engine
† batman: servant
△ FE: British plane

SIXTY TO ONE

BATTLE BRIEFING

By the end of 1917 the RFC had clawed back control of the air from the German Air Force. New planes came into service which more than matched the Albatros, notably the Sopwith Camel, the SE5A and the Bristol Fighter. The Camel, with its amazing aerobatic abilities and twin machine guns, soon became a firm favourite and logged more kills than any other aircraft in the RFC.

In 1918 the Germans planned a last desperate bid to win the war – before American troops arrived in large numbers – and air power was to be a key part of this. Under a plan called the Amerikaprogramm, aircraft production doubled to 2,000 planes a month, 24,000 new recruits were called up and the output of aviation fuel rose from 6,000 to 12,000 tons a month. By March the German Air Force had over 4,000 planes ready to support a great ground attack on the Western Front, most of them lined up against the RFC.

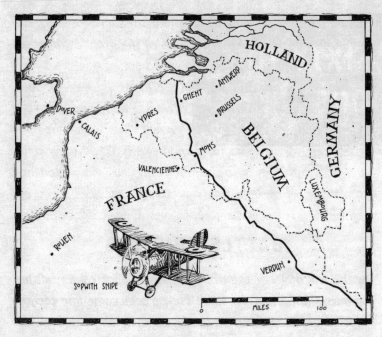

The Western Front, 1918

The assault – codenamed Operation Michael – was launched at 04:45 on 21 March with dreadful effect. Following close behind a huge bombardment, specially trained German storm troopers burst through the lines of the British Fifth Army. Four years of trench warfare came to a sudden end as the Allies were forced to make a fighting retreat. To add to the misery of the British troops, hundreds of enemy planes machine-gunned and bombed any pockets of resistance. These were the Schlastas (Battle Wings), specialized ground-attack formations, flying armoured two-seater fighters at heights of less than 325 feet (100 m).

Other units flew vital observation missions, keeping the generals informed of the progress of the ground troops, so that artillery fire could keep up with them.

For three long months the Germans pushed forward, almost reaching Amiens, and driving a wedge between the French and British armies. The French government, dreading the worst, made plans to abandon Paris. The turning point came in July. Now the German Army was exhausted and running short of supplies. It was time for the Allies, reinforced by America, to begin a series of devastating counter-attacks.

The German Air Force was better equipped, trained and supplied than ever before but the RFC, now renamed the RAF, hit back hard. British pilots fought massed air battles, grinding down the Germans and at the same time copying the tactics of the Schlastas to help their own infantry. Into this mayhem flew a skilled Canadian pilot fresh from the war in Italy – Major William Barker.

THE VISITING MAJOR

An Unwelcome Guest

The pilots of 210 Squadron were battle-hardened and weary. They had lived through the chaos of Operation Michael and suffered heavily in their dogfights with the multicoloured machines of the circuses. The last thing they needed was a Canadian tourist – however distinguished – foisted on them for a few days. OK, so he'd made his reputation fighting the Austrians on the Italian front. So what? Everyone knew Italy was a sideshow and the Austrians were pussycats compared to the Germans.

And to add insult to injury he'd grabbed one of the first Sopwith Snipes – the latest plane they were all eager to get their hands on. The rumour was it had a ceiling of 22,000 feet (96,770 m), with oxygen and an electrical heating system for the cockpit. So how come this visiting major was swanning about in one, while they had to carry on fighting with worn-out Camels! Unfair or what? The sooner he was gone the better!

The object of their scorn was Major William Barker, **DSO and Bar, MC and Two Bars**. But the pilots of

Four Sopwith Snipe Aircraft (No. 29 Squadron)

210 Squadron were more than a little unkind. Anyone who knew his record understood that Will Barker had nothing to prove.

Record of a Hero

Will was born in Dauphin, Manitoba, in 1893. He was a farm boy and a good shot with a rifle. Later, he was to show he could be every bit as accurate with a machine gun. He joined the Canadian Mounted Rifles in 1914 and spent a year in the trenches before transferring to the RFC in April 1916.

After starting as a mechanic, Will became an observer-gunner, flying in outdated BE2cs over the blood-soaked Somme. In September 1916 he and his pilot were sent out to photograph new German defences. Over enemy lines they were intercepted by two Albatros DIIs and their chances looked poor, but they inflicted so much damage on one machine that both broke off the attack. On the way back to base they were jumped again, this time fighting off four more German planes. Will was awarded his first Military Cross for this action.

In November 1916 Will was posted to England for training as a pilot. He'd gone solo after 55 minutes' flying time and gained his licence in January 1917. A month later he was back in France, this time in the cockpit of an RE8. During 'Bloody April' he flew daring observation missions, directing artillery fire on to German troops.

Major W. G. Barker beside his Sopwith Camel

On a mission in August 1917 Will was wounded by shrapnel in the side of his head and passed out from loss of blood. His observer saved the day by reviving him in time to land their plane safely.

In September Will was given a break and sent back to England to train new pilots. Here he got his first flight in a Sopwith Camel but soon grew bored with training. He wanted action. When his requests to be sent back to combat were ignored he **buzzed** Piccadilly Circus and RFC HQ. Back in France he served with 28 Squadron and ran his score up to six when he shot down two

Albatros fighters on the same day.

At the end of 1917 28 Squadron was transferred to the Italian front and over the next 10 months Will relentlessly chalked up kills – 46 enemy planes and nine balloons.

The Western Front Again

In September 1918 Will was ordered back to England, to take command of the fighter pilot training school at Hounslow, Middlesex. But once again he kicked against a job that took him away from the fighting. He argued with the top brass that he needed a short tour of duty back on the Western Front – to sharpen his skills against the latest German planes and tactics. It was clear the enemy was losing the war now, but the German Air Force remained a deadly opponent. How could he be a convincing leader if he hadn't faced the best the enemy had to offer? Reluctantly they gave in and allowed him a short, roving tour of the front. He could pick any plane and any squadron he wanted.

Will settled on 210 Squadron, based at Beugnâtre, France, because an old friend was there. The commanding officer was Major Cyril Leman, Will's pilot from the days when he was a rookie observer back in 1916. At least there would be one welcoming face for evening meals in the officers' mess.

It was just as well he had Leman to talk to. The other pilots never warmed to Will on his ten-day tour. And he did little to break the ice. He didn't drink, smoke or have much time for horseplay. He kept his own company on the ground and never flew in patrols in the air. He took off with the squadron but used the Snipe's high-altitude performance to hang hawk-like above them – hunting for targets. He was written off by the others as a bigheaded ace looking to boost his own score and reputation.

Will stayed with 210 Squadron for ten frustrating days, dogged by bad weather and bad luck. He barely saw a target, let alone got close enough for a kill. Then on 26 October the news came he had been dreading. The hunt was over. He was ordered to return the Snipe at once and report to Hounslow. Will was furious but had no choice ... except ... perhaps ...

VC Sunday

The next morning, Sunday, Will was up before dawn. The sky was brightening and the rain that had fallen all through the night had stopped. There was barely a cloud in sight. He took off for England but was determined to make one last detour – a short spin over German lines. Just in case.

Will had been in the air about 20 minutes when he noticed that a white German two-seater was doing a reconnaissance of the area. A Rumpler, he thought. It was well above him, 21,000 (6,460 m) feet or maybe even more. Jackpot. They were flying over the Mormal Forest, near Valenciennes. He glanced at his watch. It was 08:25.

Will felt a rush of excitement. If the war ended soon this might be his last chance to add to his score. Climbing steadily, he closed on the target. But he could tell this was not going to be an easy victory. The Germans were alert and well trained and they saw him coming. The Rumpler's pilot opened the throttle and manoeuvred the plane deftly so his observer could blast away at the 'Englishman'.

Wheeling and turning, the aircraft chased through the sky, each looking for an advantage. The German observer hit the Snipe several times but missed Will. Finally Will moved in from behind and a little below . . . and at a range of 600 feet (185 m) fired a burst that killed or wounded the gunner. Now, with the enemy helpless, he fired burst after burst into the cockpit, engine and wings at point-blank range. The Rumpler broke apart and one airman parachuted to safety . . . only one.

Will stared at his victim, watching the German's parachute blossom and the pieces fall. It was hypnotic, thrilling . . .

It was stupid.

Will had lost his concentration.

Wham. He felt an explosion of pain as a bullet tore into his right thigh, smashing the bone and almost severing his leg. He had turned from hunter into prey.

In the long seconds Will had taken to enjoy his

victory, a Fokker DVII had sneaked up. Climbing steeply, the German had fired a long burst that nearly finished him. Whether through shock or instinct he threw the Snipe into a steep left bank and fell away. Turning tightly, both planes dropped thousands of feet before Will out-circled the Fokker and fired a burst into its fuel tank. It vanished in a wall of flame.

The Fokker DVII

But the Canadian's problems were just beginning! As he levelled out, Will found himself flying head on into the full strength of a circus – at least 60 DVIIIs in stepped-up formation from 8,000 feet (2,460 m). For a moment the Germans were stunned. Anxious heads scanned the horizon. Was this a trap? Where were the other English aircraft? For a few brief moments nothing happened. Then the most eerie air battle of the war began – sixty to one.

Will battles for his life as the Germans line up to attack!

Will, badly wounded and without a parachute, realized there was no chance of escape. 'If I'm going to die,' he thought, 'I'll take another Hun with me.' Wheeling on the tail of a Fokker, he fired two bursts and it fell away in a spin.

Satisfied the Snipe was alone, the other Germans peeled into flights of five and took turns to attack from different sides. One flight would wheel in from above and the next from below, so that no matter how Will looped or dived he was always a target. The Snipe was chewed up by gunfire – hit over 300 times – and Will wounded again in the left hip.

Fainting from blood loss, he plunged 6,000 feet (1,840 m) in a spin, until the rush of air revived him and he pulled out of his fall. But not out of trouble! This time he had levelled out in the lower tier of the circus and the German attacks began once more. In desperation he picked the nearest enemy plane and tried to ram it, firing as he neared. Just as he reached the Fokker it blew apart and fell away. But Will paid a price – he was hit in the left arm, smashing his elbow, and as he fainted again the Snipe plunged into another spin.

This probably saved his life. The crazy, gyrating fall made it difficult for the Fokkers to follow him down and get a clear bead on the target. Incredibly, as the Snipe neared the ground, Will woke again and saw a familiar sight on the horizon: observation balloons. Straightening out, he ran at low altitude towards British lines and crash-landed at 90 mph (144 kph) near 29 Kite Balloon Section.

The balloonists rushed to the wreckage and lifted the severely injured pilot free. The cockpit was drenched in blood and one of his legs seemed to be held on by a sinew alone. Will was rushed by motor tender to a field dressing station and then on to 8 General Hospital in Rouen. Doctors fought for hours to save his life and he was unconscious for 10 days.

On 11 November the Great War came to an end – and on 20 November Will Barker was awarded the Victoria Cross. The citation read:

This combat, in which Major Barker destroyed four enemy machines (three of them in flames), brought his total success to fifty three enemy machines destroyed, and is a notable example of the exceptional bravery and disregard of danger which this very gallant officer has always displayed throughout his distinguished career.

FIGHTING FACTS

What Really Happened on 27 October?

The version of Will Barker's action you have just read is commonly accepted, but doubts have been raised by his latest biographer, Wayne Ralph.

- **Doubt 1** All the independent witnesses were on the ground and couldn't have seen what happened in detail.
- **Doubt 2** The combat report was written by Major Leman, the commanding officer of 210 Squadron, not Will himself. Will never gave a detailed account of the fight, except to say, 'I was severely injured and shot down.'
- **Doubt 3** Will's story became big news and an exaggerated legend. It's difficult to pick apart a fable

once it has gripped the public imagination.

- **The Big Doubt** The fuselage of Will's Snipe was shipped out to Canada in 1919 and was on display until 1996. It shows little evidence of being torn apart by enemy bullets. Wayne Ralph doubts that Will fought a full circus or shot down four enemy planes. Even so, he credits him with one kill and one probable kill and doesn't doubt his courage or that he tangled with a large formation of enemy planes. His book argues that William Barker should be remembered for his whole remarkable flying career, rather than just the VC episode.

Severe Wounds

Will never fully recovered from his wounds, though he lived on till 1930 and flew again. He had been hit by high velocity, 7.92-mm bullets travelling at more than 2,500 feet (770 m) per second. These tumble in the air, increasing the damage when they hit a body. The shock wave generated in front of each bullet and the **cavitation** behind force human tissue to stretch and recoil some distance from the wound track. Angry Allied pilots wrongly accused the Germans of using explosive bullets.

Courageous Camel

Will shot down most of his kills flying the same plane in Italy – a Sopwith Camel B6313. Even when his squadron all changed to the excellent Bristol FE2, Will hung on to his Camel. It logged more than 379 hours of flight time and became the single most successful aircraft in the war. B6313 was retired from service and dismantled on 2 October 1918.

Parachute Problems

Will Barker couldn't escape by parachute after he was injured on 27 October – *because he didn't have one!* Yet as early as the 1880s parachutes had been shown to work, with circus showmen using them jumping from balloons at a great height and landing safely. By 1917, French, German and US pilots were all equipped with 'chutes. Even British balloonists had them – but not the RFC.

R. E. Calthorpe, a retired British engineer, had developed a compact parachute nicknamed 'the Guardian Angel' before the war. He told the RFC about his invention and successful tests were carried out at the Royal Aircraft Factory at Farnborough. Despite good results, Sir David Henderson, Commander of the Royal Flying Corps, refused to issue them. Two main arguments were used against them, one practical and one moral:

- Even the Guardian Angel was too bulky and heavy, and therefore likely to affect the performance of an aircraft.
- Nothing should be done to 'impair the fighting spirit of pilots and cause them to abandon machines which might otherwise be capable of returning to base for repair'.

Aces like Mick Mannock were driven wild by the

Kite balloon observers preparing to descend by parachute

arrogant stupidity of the 'top brass' ... and hundreds of pilots died needlessly.

Lessons Forgotten

The RFC grew from a tiny band of pilots into the finest air force on the Allied side, with over 22,000 aircraft in service by 1918. No longer underpowered string bags fit only for watching armies on the ground, planes had become fast, reliable and deadly. And the pace of change did not slacken. By the middle of World War II, barely 25 years later, aircraft were capable of devastating enemy cities and grinding armies to a halt. Crucially, the atomic bombs that brought that war to an end were dropped from the air.

266

Favourite Mess Song of the Lafayette Escadrille, a Unit of American Pilots Flying with the French Air Force

We meet 'neath the sounding rafters,
The walls all around us are bare;
They echo the peals of laughter;
It seems that all the dead are there.

So stand by your glasses steady,
This world is a world of lies.
Here's a toast to the dead already;
Hurrah for the next man who dies.

Cut off from the land that bore us,
Betrayed by the land that we find,
The good men have gone before us,
And only the dull are left behind,

So stand by your glasses steady,
The world is a web of lies.
Then here's to the dead already,
And hurrah for the next man who dies.

RFC LINGO

ace a pilot with a large number of kills. The highest-scoring British ace was Edward Mannock with 73.

Archie anti-aircraft fire. The explanation is complicated! A London show in 1914 had a song in which a young lady stopped her boyfriend from smooching with the catchphrase 'Not now, Archie.' One pilot used to yell this every time his plane came under fire . . . and pretty soon it caught on.

Beware the Hun in the sun! look out for enemy planes attacking out of the sun. This made them hard to spot. Pilots needed rubber necks.

Boche nickname for a German

buzzed flew very low over

ceiling the highest a plane can reach.

CO commanding officer.

dogfight a shoot-out in the air.

Hun unsavoury nickname for a German, after the barbaric Huns of history.

joystick control lever that could be operated with one hand.

pusher aircraft with rear-mounted engine and propeller.

sausages observational balloons with elongated gasbags.

scout a fast single-seater plane, originally designed for quick reconnaissance flights. These became the aircraft sent up to intercept enemy machines. By 1918 'scout' had come to mean the same as 'fighter' today.

scrambled ordered to get into the plane.

tractor aircraft with front-mounted engine and propeller.

witches' water gasoline. It was given the nickname because many pilots burnt to death when their fuel ignited.

GLOSSARY

Alleyman a German. Taken from the French for Germany, *Allemagne*

amphibious attack an assault from the sea

batteries fortified emplacements for heavy artillery

belligerents countries at war

billets somewhere to rest, perhaps with a Belgian family or at least a dry tent

bridgehead ground captured from the enemy after an attack from the sea

butts targets

cavitation low pressure

cenotaph war memorial or memorial to someone buried elsewhere. Cenotaph is Greek for 'empty tomb'

coaming raised edging to keep the wind out

collaborator native of an occupied country, such as Belgium or France, working for the Germans

commandeered seized by the army. The civilian owners were paid compensation

Communist Revolution revolution to overthrow the Russian monarch, the Tsar, and to improve the lives of the people

conscripts soldiers who are ordered to join the army by the government

cowling engine cover

cut daisies to skim very low to the ground

'Deutschland, Deutschland über Alles' the German national anthem

Dominions self-governing colonies of the British Empire

drum a round magazine of bullets for quick loading into a machine gun

DSO and Bar, MC and Two Bars Will Barker had an impressive array of medals, the Distinguished Service Order and the Military Cross. A bar is a strip of silver below the clasp of a medal, to show the wearer has been recognized for bravery again

dugout a rough shelter, often dug into the side of a trench. Sometimes referred to as a funkhole

elevators control surface used to climb or dive in an aircraft or airship

fire steps the ledges cut for soldiers to stand on and fire at the enemy

fuselage body of a plane

guncotton nitrocellulose, an explosive

Houdinis Harry Houdini was a magician who specialized in great escapes

internment camp prison camp for enemy civilians

jam on full aileron and rudder set the controls to turn the plane over

Kaiser German emperor and war leader

a kill shooting down or forcing an enemy plane to land, not necessarily killing the enemy crew

Landsturm part-time German reserve soldiers, a bit like the Home Guard in World War II

Lewis gun a light, reliable machine gun

machined the cylinder heads modified the engine to increase the power

manoeuvres war-training exercises

Mills bomb grenade

mobilize to gather an army together

NCO non-commissioned officer. A soldier from the ranks, appointed to lead others – like a corporal or sergeant

neutral to not take sides in the war

nocturnal active at night

oilskin waterproof coat

orderlies attendants in military hospitals, cleaning and doing basic nursing work

outflank get behind and cut off part of the enemy army

parapets bank or wall to protect soldiers from enemy fire

phosgene poisonous gas used by both sides. It had a nasty delayed action, causing sudden death as long as two days after exposure. It was common for a victim not to realize he had been gassed

POWs prisoners of war

put on rudder turned sharply

quicklime caustic calcium oxide powder, used as a disinfectant

resistance movement civilians organizing opposition to the conquering power

safe house property that was safe from the enemy, where fugitives could be hidden

salient the front line sticking out into enemy territory

sally ports holes cut in the sides of ships to let the troops out

sapper a private in the Royal Engineers

skirmish small battle

Tommies German nickname for British soldiers

U-boat German submarine. Taken from *Unterseeboot*, the German for 'under-sea boat'

ACKNOWLEDGEMENTS

Part 1: Stories from the Land

Many thanks to Richard Racey for permission to retell his
father's amazing escape story and for his kindness in checking
the manuscript.

'My Boy Jack' by Rudyard Kipling by permission of A. P. Watt
Ltd on behalf of The National Trust for Places of Historical
Interest or Natural Beauty.

Picture Credits
IWM: p. 11, Q2314; p. 21, Q70165; p. 31, Q44172;
p. 45, Q6209; p. 59, Q61088; p. 64–5, 25142; p. 77, Q24050;
p. 78, HU83790; p. 79, Q48451; p. 95, Q79836;
p. 102, Q15064B; p. 113, Q106364; p. 115, Q33161

Mary Green's Picture Library: p. 20

BPK: p. 39

Hulton Getty: p. 121, 122, 123

Part 2: Stories from the Air

Thanks to George Tones, for checking the technical spec. on the aircraft.

W. B. Yeats: 'An Irish Airman Foresees His Death' from *Collected Poems* by W. B. Yeats, by permission of A. P. Watt Ltd on behalf of Michael B. Yeats.

The Royal Air Force Benevolent Fund is a charity that provides assistance to those of the extended RAF family who need support. Look at www.rafbf.org for more details.

TRACEY TURNER

HOW CAN A PIGEON Be a War Hero?

Why did the First World War start?

Did soldiers still fight
with swords?

Had aeroplanes been invented yet?

Find out the answers to these and lots
of other exciting questions in this
brilliantly informative book, which will
tell you everything you ever needed to
know about the First World War.